LEARNING BEHAVIORAL ECONOMY EDITON 2

JOHN LOK

Contents

Foreword

Introduction

This book is concerned ro explain why business organizations must need to cocern social responsibilty. I shall indicate some different marketing and economy and organizational behavioural theories or concepts how to solve the USA actual organizations' challenges in the situations. Also I shall compare to explain what advantages and disadvantages between any one of my solvable suggestions and the any one of the company's choice of solvable method to any one of these case study challenges to aim to let any reader to judge whether how to choose the solvable method is better. This book is one teaching book to give some business concepts how to apply to solve the individual company's actual case studies challenges. Theories include: online knowledgeable concept, globalization job concept , useful indicator concept, standard growth enhancing policy, standard growth enhancing policy, outsourcing, national environment policy, tax policy, production orientation and societal marketing orientation, segmentation, existence needs (E), relatedness needs (R) and growth needs (G) psychological concepts etc.

The first part, I shall explain what the labour economy concept is. I shall indicate evidences to give my reasons to predict knowledgeable jobs, such as online office workers, online freelance electronic book authors, online survey researcher, online business researcher etc. internet channel office jobs which will be caused popularly in the future. So, I shall indicate why employers need to concern this online job issue because nowadays employees prefer to work free time and no overtime often.

In second part, it shall indicate how the process of behaviour economic field develops, then I shall show what methods are used to measure behavioural economy. Next, I shall indicate what the main two categories of behavioural economy are as well as I shall explain what risky and uncertain outcomes of individual behavior economic theories are as well as what behavioral game theory is. Finally, I shall explain behavioral economic principles of policy makers or decision makers as well as I shall also analyze whether behavioral economy and psychology which has close relationship. This book is suitable to any economists or policy makers or individual consumption makers or students or working people who have interest learn how to apply behavioural economy to judge to do the most reasonable or the most right economic activities in everyday life.

In third part, I shall let reader can learn how to use policy to solve economic challenges. I shall analyse the processes from this aspects. Such as, human development policy, tax policy, educational development policy, national environment protection policy, regulatory managment policy, private invement encouragement policy, behavioral economy and psychology leadership policy. I also indicate example and cases to explain why these policies can be applied to assist economic growth to any countries for long term.

Prologue

Table of contents

- The two categories of behavioral economy.

- Explanation what are of Preferences over risky and uncertain outcomes of individual behavior economic theories.
    - What is behavioral game theory?

- What are Behavioral economic principles of policy makers or decision makers ?
    - Analysis whether behavioral economy and psychology which has close relationship.
    - What are labor economy and behavioral economy difference
    - The historical development of behavioral economics and function is.
    - The methods of measurement to behavioral economics.
    - Explanation what are of Preferences over risky and uncertain outcomes of individual behavior economic theories.
    - What is behavioral game theory?
    - What are Behavioral economic principles of policy makers or decision makers ?
    - Analysis whether behavioral economy and psychology which has close relationship.

What is time series perspective on economic growth to pursue for growth and human development strategies.

What is quantitative evidence to review policy to reduce the threats from economic recession risk occurrence.

Regulatory management method

Whether it has relationship between political instability and national economic performance.

Tax policy influences, during polictical instability environment.

What is educational development policy

What is national environment policy

How government policy can influence on capturing private investment.

Whether national leadership and economic growth has close relationship.

Whether behavioral economy and psychology knowledge can be applied to assist economic development.

Bibliography

ONE

WHY DOES ONLINE KNOWLEDGEABLE JOBS WILL BE RAISED PRODUCTIVITY

In what way has globalization affected employers choose online work to provide to local or overseas to raise productivity? Is online work still a useful working place environment for local and overseas employers to raise productivity in a globalized online age, such as online electronic books' authors, online office administration or online surveys or online researchers etc. kind of online jobs supplying? Our age is entering an online business environment, such as online electronic air tickets sale, online electronic books publishing, online advertising and online shopping and website design service promotion , online university education etc. different kind of online businesses from internet. It seems online channel can increase global online job chances to affect that our live and our job nature to be changed every day. For example, online electronic book publishing business will be popular, many different countries' readers who like to buy electronic books to study, due to these online electronic book shops, e.g. Amazon, lulu, book Rix, book tango etc. electronic book stores which can provide free charge to deliver cheaper paper books to any overseas countries' readers' homes and which paper book prices are more cheaper to compare to book shops' paper books process after who have paid to buy any electronic books or paper books from these online book stores websites. Moreover, these readers can read these book stores' electronic books from online publishing sellers' websites to download these electronic books to study at homes or any libraries etc. computer provision of places easily and conveniently. So readers do not need to walk to any book shops to buy any paper books and who also do not need to bring any heavy paper books back to homes conveniently. Hence, electronic publishers can provide electronic book authors' job chances to write their books and type to computers to register to be online authors to publish whose electronic or paper books to earn loyalty income at home very easily. Also, the globalizing online job nature can change the customized office work style. It won't need staffs go to office to work from 9:00 AM to 6:00 PM. In general office workers need to spend eight to ten working hours with five or six working days within per week commonly. Hence, online office workers don't need to pay transportation fee and lunch cost, due who can work at their home when who turn on their computer to enter whose employers' websites to work and make email communication to connect between them conveniently. So, I feel the online electronic book authors and online office administration jobs which will be popular further occupations to be provided from global online job structure style and many labors will like to work online, then who can raise productivity conveniently when who work at home in the future. Beside, due to online (internet) is very popular and cheap cost to be needed to spend expenditure from employer. So, internet will build the relationships between workplaces and every staff role identity and everyday life and online working environments can connect them to work in the process of globalization in the future. Also, our everyday life and work is entering in a globalizing world. It emphasizes on time and space compression and the importance of virtual space and experience in our daily lives of many people, the working style seems spent online working time to change how our social traditional work roles and our traditional office working places-based environments to home online working environments further long time in the future. So, employers ought plan to prepare online working methods to let their employees to raise productivity. In conclusion, Online knowledgeable concept can raise productivity because many office jobs can be accepted to apply online technological working in order to reduce staff numbers and to raise fast speed job efficiency.

Why does knowledgeable online jobs will raise economic growth?

Social science can explain knowledgeable jobs will be useful and popular and assisting labors to raise productivity to work at home online working environments. Within social science, in such discipline is sociology and human psychology and geography which indicates internet technology have changed to online working place environment, sense of working place, online employee role identity, everyday online work and life style, website global working communication and email online communication working interconnections. It seems internet brings access to social, economic and political resources to effect change to both individual and social working conditions, such as employers accept to attempt to use internet to assist office staffs to work at home, e.g. many book publishing businesses like to attempt to publish electronic books from online book store, instead of book shops channel to sell paper books. So these online book stores give chance to authors to publish electronic books or online paper books from online sale channel to earn loyalty income. For example, Amazon online electronic bookstore can publish electronic books and online paper books to sell all one day 24 hours to any countries' readers from its website, so when any countries' readers can enter its website to choose any different kind of subjects of electronic books to buy by visa card conveniently. Such as fiction, psychology, economy, science, law, architecture, medicine, commerce, management etc. subjects. So, any country's reader who does not need to buy air tickets to go to the country's book shop to buy the paper book, who only needs to pay visa card to buy the electronic or online paper books from Amazon publishing's website to buy any countries' electronic and paper books and then the overseas reader can choose either to download it from whose home computer or pays more price to deliver the online paper book to post to whose country conveniently. Hence, this online bookstore sale method will be popular and many free work authors will choose to work to raise the productivity of more quality electronic books numbers from this internet channel.

However, the consequences of global change are far from uniform with globalizing influences and adapted as new technological, economic and online working cultural experiences are incorporated by any countries' staffs of any cities, towns and rural areas into their everyday work lives from long distance easily. Since one company can employ different countries' staffs to work from internet working channel at their homes. For example, a America company can employ overseas countries' staffs to work at the same time together by sending job duties from email communication channel among them when the America company has any job arrangement to notify to any staff to finish it any time, then the overseas staff finish the job and who can send whose finished documents to whose America employer any time. It seems the overseas staffs whose working hours can be flexible and those working hours have no regular office working hours to be fixed time table, so they do not need to work in any fixed working time table every working days, who can send their finished office documents to whose employers after who have finished their documents by either email communication channel or office online website downloads office download any time conveniently.

It will be a new working style position that online working globalization is in a new stage. We are living in an age of very rapid and fluid flow of information, ideas, products and people which are having an effect of a variety of scales. I shall indicate evidences to explain why employers will encounter online knowledgeable jobs to raise productivity in a globalizing world by sociology concept. I shall focus on research into the connections between our everyday online life style, online working place and online working role identity. The first is that everyday online life is the manifestation of social existence and always involves either distant or direct interaction with other people. Such as we can use internet email channel to communicate with overseas friends or strange people, even employers or employees can also use email to exchange to receive and send their office documents by email or company website any time conveniently. Good example includes such things are as online participation in work, employment, cultural events, and recreation, shopping and communication from internet channel. It is related to employees are working in whose home working places and their home working place are possible to connect their overseas employers' offices and however, readily these may be separated in far distant conceptual terms, such as an online working environment. The employee's home is such whose employer's office, who can work at home from online channel conveniently. When who receives whose employer's email about what job duties who needs to do every day. Then, who sees his employer's email, then either if who did not understand how to do whose job duties clearly, who can send email back to ask whose employers to explain how who needs to do whose office job duties by email communication channel again easily. Even after who finish whose office job duties on that day or another day, then who can send finished office job duties to whose employers by email conveniently. In this view, online working places and sense of online working places are produced by different countries‘ large enterprise employers and overseas employees interacting together. At the same time, employees and employers whose sense are contacted by employees' individual role identity from email or office website communication channel any time. Thus, traditional office working environment is constrained and enabled by different countries‘ working histories and cultures and social class backgrounds and economic conditions and job opportunities, working positions of power and working geographical locations and development of local change and distant social interaction. In the future, online working place will be changed from traditional socially significant to online social relationship; underlying this sense of online working place will be the notion that some employers and employees themselves ought feel that life. Moreover, online working place is the possibility of non controlling employees' working time, due to working hours are flexible and employers‘ working places sizes are very limited to supply to many staffs to work in a limited office working place in the same working time. It seems online home environment will be very popular, due to every employee will use whose home to work to finish whose office documents at home every day any time very conveniently as well as employers won't need to spend much expenditure to pay for large sizes of office rent when the employer needs to rent more than one room office at more than one floor in one building. Hence, company's website expenditure can reduce the employers' office rent seriously. Moreover, employees can be dominated by feelings towards changing general office working place to online working at home as well as changing fixed working time table to flexible working time table, e.g. the staff can see whose employer's email to know what office job duties who needs to do tonight, so who will finish whose office documents and will send whose finished office documents to whose employer by email tomorrow. So, home online working environment is seen as an ideal home working place, and home online working environment which is quiet, safe and it has certain valued facilities and home online working environment is such as the type of residents in the employee's living building. This sense of living and online work place will be held by residents who will be employed in professional/ managerial/ technical etc. occupations. Hence, local employees won't catch any transportation to go to office as well as overseas employees won't also catch planes to go to whose employer's country's office to work, due to who can use online email communication or office website communication channels to work together conveniently. However, working facilities will be one online computer working commodity which is purchasable, useable and exchangeable and saleable to any employees are located at home and employers are located at office, and after a flexible working time table is discarded easily by employer, due to whose website or office email can receive any employee's individual finished office documents by every employee's individual email communication any time very conveniently. Moreover, home online working place is also like a stage on every employee's life is lived out. The employee will feel that whose life and working time is lived at home together at the same time. Similar to feel commodity sense of home and the working place which are the same location, but it is distinguished from it by the establishment of arriving strange and far distant of the employee's local or overseas employer's office when the employee's working place is family interacting to the employee's house or home.

Our world is entering globalization, people are connecting in an increasing number of ways. It is clear also that is the face of globalization, the ways of our everyday working life is either constituted which are still shaped by local expenditure of working place or is by where the firm's overseas employees love locally, regionally and nationally or is by the access who have limited to office resources and home office online working locations opportunity changing from general office working environment to home online working environment. Roberston (1992) shows is that" this is not just about economic processes, but about social and cultural issues are as well. In the early part of the 21 ST century, it is necessary to see this as a set of processes that encompass economic, political, social, cultural and environmental changes." In conclusion, online knowlegeable concept can raise economic growth because many clients accept online shopping, so the GDP from overseas sale numbers will increase any gross domestic products.

Why employers need to considerate the low
income level worker whose living of standard challenge.

Is globalization influenced to new online knowledgeable jobs to be provided to raise low income level worker's living od standard? One of the key areas of debate among theorists is the extent to which globalization is a new phenomenon or stage in a process. When it began and the path that it has followed and thus how new it is. Such as internet is used in communication aspect in early, e.g. hospital or war email communication channel. Then, many businessmen discovered online electronic commerce is also one online sale and purchase method. So, it will cause online office workers or online freelance online jobs, e.g. electronic book authors working style or electronic book reading cultural existed in our society in common possibly in the future. However, I recognize globalization is a misleading concept since what is described as globalization has been happening for the 500 years history ago. Rather what is new is that human are entering an age of transition, such as online knowledgeable workers or knowledgeable nature of different jobs will be caused from online working environment popularly. There are key processes of globalization: the economic, often is seen as the central process, the political, social, cultural and online working environment. Every natural economy needs to maintain the rate of growth, employment, welfare provision and minimum wage balance levels, so it will cause knowledgeable jobs provided, such as online organized labors, it also will change the traditional office organizational environment to cause online new organizational home work environment popularly in the future. Hence, economic and political has close connection, political and cultural has also close connection, cultural and social has also close connection, social and working environment has also connection. After all these connections cause globalization finally, then the new online knowledgeable working environment, such as online jobs will be required by global office employees popularly in the future. It will bring many online workers supply to the employment market in the future. As capital in the new globalized economy has a limited attachment to working place, production centers, such as offices, factories or farms which locate any where it is competitively advantages to do so, and economic activity moves to where labor is cheapest or raw materials is the least expensive. It can be raised demand to online knowledgeable workers demand in global competitive employment environment directly. For example, cultural, social, global expansion of Mc Donald's and other fast food chains will be entered to the online sale channel. Hence, environmental globalization raises human awareness, includes a new view of the natural and the social worlds to environmental protection message. These message source is from online channel popularly nowadays. Online organizing environment and living will influence our everyday working worlds. Due to many industrial cities and life will be not needed by global employers. However, industrial cities concentrate on demanding in developing countries, e.g. China, India, Korea etc. countries. So, developed countries, such as America, England, Japan etc. countries' employers will need many online knowledgeable employees to help them to work from online work place environment popular in the future. Later, knowledgeable online working environment will be popular to developing countries when which economy had developed mature in the future. So, it is possible online jobs will raise low income level householders' living of standard because online can create more job chance for this group people.

Can a useful indicator measure income living standard to assist economic growth?

Nowadays, developing countries, such as India, China, Hong Kong, etc. and developed countries, such as America, England etc. which are facing social challenges. For example, many low income level householders whose income level can't be raised and inflation is also high in society. Although, these developing countries' economy is growing, but which can not raise the low income level householders' income level to let them have afford to buy one house in minimum in whose country, even these low income level family have no enough income to buy foods to eat and cloths to wear easily. Also, the developed countries‘ economy had arrived the mature growing stage, but which also can not give any benefits to whose low level income level income householders group. Hence, governments have responsibilities to find methods to solve these challenges, such as: How to reduce poor occurrence? How much does economic growth help the poor? How can social policy help? Can a country have a sizeable low-wage sector of house to provide to the poor? What role can public service social spending better for the poor?

Justice is the distribution of income and wealth is fairest. Any country's government needs play a large role in determining it's citizen's abilities to do common occupation, what job choices are preferences to them, how to raise employment of motivation and what social circumstances are to cause households have no poor occurrence to cause many low level income jobs to do to earn income in society. In order to reduce the unfair income distribution between rich and poor people. Why it is important to improve unfair income treatment between rich and poor people to any countries? However, in a rich and growing economic country, such as America, England etc. , which are difficult to justify stagnant living standards for those at the floor bottom low income people nowadays. Although, these developed countries' economy are growing, but which can not give benefits to this low level income households group. However, I suggest any country ought favor not simply a satisfactory level of living standards for the poor people, but it ought consider how to improve or review poor people living standards every year. Analysts typically set the poverty line at 50 or 60 percent of the median income within each country. In general, poverty means to level of resources insufficient to achieve a minimal acceptable standard of living as well as people tends to experience poverty as relative is to living standards by comparison in any country's citizen's own society. If the absolute incomes or living standards for the poor grow less rapidly than those of households in the middle income level in the country. So, it seems that it is not fair economic growth in these developing countries and income seems to be a useful indicator to measure living of standard.

How to apply " standard growth enhancing policy" to improve low income level householders living of standard to raise productivity

Is income a useful indicator of living standards? Income is a resource that allows any country's households to acquire the sort of things e.g. food, housing, medical care, transportation, education, entertainment etc. needs. So, which are needed for a minimal decent standard of living. Income also is comparatively easy to measure. However, causing poor factors might have many reasons, such as illness, temporary unemployment, a large amount of bonus reduction, overtime long time working hours, family members unemployment, even economic decline (falling down), so these factors can reduce jobs supply to any countries to cause poor occurrence. However, any countries' income measures seldom include the value of government service and in kind benefit, such as pension, unemployment assistance etc. as well as some low income households have assets (savings in bank, and owned home). So, it seems income is not an accurate measure to the actual living standard to the low income people numbers in the countries effectively. If income is not an accurate measure to actual living standard, then it can not improve the low income level householders of living standard and productivity level will be reduced because these low income level labors can not get reasonable salaries and unfair welfare to work from whose employers. Otherwise, the high income level labors can get increased salaries and fair welfare to work from whose employers. When these both low and high income level labors work in same company, the low income level labors will feel angry to work unhappy, then it is possible that who will decrease their productivity.

The poor people numbers will be reduced possibly. How to evaluate the actual poor people numbers decreasing? In think when the degree to the country which economic growth boosts the income level of low and households to rise their general savings amounts to the income level of middle households. Then, the country's poor people numbers will be decreasing, due to this group of the numbers of incomes level of low households has been decreasing and it's numbers has been increasing to the income level of middle group, then productivity will also raise to every employers in any country.

In general, economic growth is assumed that poor households get more jobs, work more hours and/or receives higher wages. Hence, when one country measure economic growth, which can apply the relationship between per capita GDP and low income households of numbers between the past year and current year to measure the rising or falling numbers per capita GDP in the low and income households group, for example, in Sweden, Denmark, Norway, the Netherlands and Finland countries which net transfers are received by low income level households increased significantly between 1979 year and 2007 year. But, average earnings, were flat in Demarks country, when in Sweden and Finland countries which declined sharply during those countries' deep recessions in the early 1990 year. Otherwise, in the United Kingdom, the period was from 1979 year to 1995 year, it saw no changes in transfers pension or retirement savings from United Kingdom government and a slight drop in earnings, but from 1999 year to 2005 year, social earning increased slightly, but more important was a large rise in net government pension and retirement saving transfers, which resulted in a sizeable increase in low income level incomes group. When net government pension or retirement savings transfers to citizen increased this was caused by economic growth. In general, economic growth allows policy makers to boost inflation-adjusted benefit levels for pension or retirement saving transfer to citizen programs, which will increased the incomes of pension or retirement saving benefit recipients. With GDP rising, government social benefit pension or retirement saving transfers as a share of GDP tended to remark more or less constant.

However, in some countries, the rise in pension of retirement saving net transfers was achieved in part by reduction of income or profit taxes for low income households or low business profit households, since the 1970 year, most of the world's rich nations, such as America, united Kingdom have not significantly increased the share of their GDP that goes to pensions or retirement savings transfer for the low income level poor households. It seems that if any country hoped the low income level of householders numbers will be increase, which ought need to upgrade their low income level to go up middle income level in society, then its economic growth will be raising. How economic growth can boost incomes for the poor households. It seems economic growth has made rising low income level of households is more likely, but several countries are exceptions. They experienced growing per capita GDP, but little or no improvement in the income of low income level of households, such as Hong Kong has seven million people who are living in a small city. Although, it was encountering economic growth from 1970 year in beginning, but the low income level of households had little or no improvement, it was possible that the numbers of Hong Kong low income level of households are more than the middle or high income level of households seriously. So, the HK economic growth seems not improve low income level of households to assist this low income level of households to raise whose income to be risen to the middle income level of households group. The reason is possible that the failure of some governments to increase public transfers as the economy grows is a key part of reason. But why did not more economic growth reach the low income level of poor households in the form of rising market income? For example, in HK, whether economic growth is likely to directly benefit the poor group's employment hours reduction and rising hourly wage levels. However, I discovered that HK economic growth produced no increase in the wage or salary market rate of low level of income households and without employment hours reduction and without rising hourly wage levels. So, HK economic growth seems to raise more job supply in the employment market, but it seems without employment hours reduction. Otherwise, it's economic growth rises employment hours, but without rising hourly wage. Hence, it seems low income level householders of numbers and economic growth have close relationship to any country, so employers need to concern their labors numbers of low income level to raise their income to be middle income level in society.

Why economists need to concern ethic to raise producticity
I recommend this economic policy to reduce poor occurrence, such as growth on average benefit the poor as much as anyone lives in the country's society, such as "standard growth enhancing policy" should be at the center of any poverty reduction strategy. I believe economic growth is the most powerful instrument for reducing poverty, due to many businessmen have enough money to invest to their countries to do any kind of businesses, then the jobs supply will be raised any many people can get any jobs supply number is more than job seekers number, then it is no doubt, the unemployment numbers will be reduced. When many people have new jobs to do and who can earn enough wages to prepare to save more money in bank.

What has been the impact of economic growth on employment hours and wages? In fact, work hours are matter a great deal for the incomes of poor group of households in developed countries, such as United States or United Kingdom or developing countries, such as Hong Kong, China etc. countries. For example, HK economic growth has a large influence to raise employment hours more than rising wage levels, such as HK general working hours are risen up to 10 to 12 hours or more per week working days to low income level of households, but the low income level of households group has not been rising wage level generally. So, I feel HK economic growth could not give any benefits to the low income level of households, such as without reduction employment hours and without raising wage level to the low income level of households in HK. Also, HK's economic growth only raises many jobs supply in HK society. Otherwise, America economic growth can give benefits to low income level of households, such as reduction employment hours, rising wage level to low income level of households and raising jobs supply in America society. Hence, the developed countries, such as America , England which economic growth can give more benefits to low income level of households. Otherwise, the developing countries, such as India, China, Korea which economic growth can not give more benefits to the low income level of households and these developing countries will cause disadvantages to this low income level of poor group in society. It is possible that the developing countries' low income level of households often need to increase to spend more working hours to assist whose employers to develop whose employers' business, due to their employers do not want to increase to employ extra workers or staffs to assist whose business development, who need whose current employees to raise more extra working hours to work to raise work efficiency when these developing countries are encountering the economic growth stage.

For example, HK employers do not concern moral issues about abnormal working hours influence. The outcome is either Hong Kong labors work long time working hours abnormally who can not rise Hong Kong economic growth or who can rise Hong Kong economic growth in long time. Generally, Hong Kong employers choose to pay less salary expenditure to need many extra labors to work abnormal working hours to help them to rise productivity, but who don't concern that long time working factor will influence unhealthy to current workers due to who need to work long time working hours abnormally in long time and it seems to cause their workers will reduce productivity and inefficiency in long time.

Although, it is possible that HK labors can be increased extra abnormal working hours to work to rise Hong Kong employers' productivity and assist HK social economy will be grown up in short term, but it is also possible that it can't rise Hong Kong economic growth due to their unhealthy or sick increasing to cause productivity declining and inefficiency in long time. Thus, I shall find evidence to analyze whether Hong Kong labors need to work abnormal long time working hours. Otherwise, who will decline Hong Kong economic growth and reduce productivity and inefficiency in long time as well as I shall give suggestion to indicate whether either current workers work abnormal long time working hours or employers ought choose to employ more extra part time workers to assist current labors to rise their productivity to decide which is the best choice to raise HK economic growth and efficient productivity in long time.

Effects on Hong Kong employment of working time reduction is found to be difficult to predict. The results of Hong Kong macroeconomic simulations of the effects on employments of working time reduction rely heavily on certain basic assumptions, such as how many hours people will actually work or how productivity and pay levels will develop. Whether HK abnormal working hours will assist HK social economic growth or economic falling down in long term.

The reasons cause Hong Kong labors who need to work abnormal long time working hours. In fact, it isn't the reason that the Hong Kong high skillful labors market is shortage to supply for the nature of some occupations, e.g.

hospital doctors and nurses, university teachers, law firm lawyers etc. professional occupations. HK has many high qualification university students graduation, it has enough labor supply to high labor market every year. The reason is that employers don't like to spend more salary to increase to employ extra labors to share current workers workload, such as low skillful and hardworking labors, such as cleaners, securities, waiters and high skillful professionals, such as hospital doctors and nurses, university teachers, lawyers etc. However, the low and high skillful labor market can be enough supply in Hong Kong, but Hong Kong employers need the current high and low both skillful workers who need to work more than 10 to 12 hours or more per working day commonly. It is possible that HK high and low educational labors will be caused unhealthy and lack enough sleep if who still need to work abnormal working hours time in long time. Although, who can rise productivity and efficiency in the short time, but it is possible that who can't rise productivity and inefficiency in the long time. Moreover, it will cause many young or middle or old ages high educational or low educational knowledgeable hardworking workers who will lose many jobs provided and who will be hard to find any jobs in HK labor employment market if HK employers don't choose to pay extra salaries to employ extra full time workers to share current labors' workload in the high and low salary occupations, due to they only choose to increase abnormal additional extra working hours to current workers to achieve to reduce employment expenditure and raise productivity. Hence, it is possible to influence HK social economy grows up slowly, even it's economy can go down seriously in long time.

I shall assume that working wage or salary of every

individual labors can not be increased, even can be decreased as well as whose normal working hours can be increased abnormally in generally. This means that the Hong Kong individual worker's income will be decreased and general productivity raising is not affected generally, due to HK employers need current labors to work abnormal extra working hours to attempt to raise productivity daily, but their salary or wage have not increased more. However, HK employers need many workers to accomplish the same amount of work, even who don't like to employ extra labors to assist current workers to achieve long term productivity raising in their companies. These abnormal working hours labors will feel unfair treatment, due to they need to work abnormal working hours, but their salary or wage have not been increased.

In the first scenario of my hypothesis is about that HK labor employment market's general salary or wage has not been increased to the normal proportion of the increased extra abnormal working time(hours). Then, in HK labors market, due to the numbers of labors supply is more than the jobs supply because HK employers don't like to pay more salary or wage expenditure to employ extra labor, but they like to increase extra abnormal working hours to current workers to aim to achieve productivity. So it will cause many HK job seekers with adequate qualifications or with less qualifications who won't find any jobs easily, then the HK the numbers of unemployed people will be increased and their household incomes will decrease to cause many HK household do not like to spend easily. The result will cause a negative effect on HK social private consumption will be decreased and the businessmen' income will be decreased also. So, HK people private consumption decreasing will influence HK economy growth to be slow, even it will cause

HK economy declining in the long time.

In the second scenario of my hypothesis is about that Hong Kong workers are fully compensated for the increasing extra abnormal working time(hours) by the abnormal additional working hours calculation. Although, Hong Kong companies' productivity will be raised, but which are not to the extent that it compensates Hong Kong enterprises for their increased wage or salary costs. In fact, Hong Kong enterprises, their costs are passed on to the clients, it causes Hong Kong's economic growth has an impact on international competitiveness to cause economic declining in possible when these enterprises need to raise their products' sale prices to balance their salary or wage cost raising to win their import competitors. Another effect is that Hong Kong individual labor's incomes decrease, which means that Hong Kong private consumption also falls in this scenario to influence HK economic growth seriously. Thus, the HK economic growth problem will be caused, due to these factors lead to a fall in Hong Kong social household private consumption. Consequently, it will cause many HK employers hope to raise Hong Kong productivity and they will raise the total amount of Hong Kong labor actually worked hours will be risen to such as extent as the increasing in normal working time(hours) from 8 or 9 hours per normal working day to 10 or 11 or 12 hours, even more extra abnormal hours per working day to the current labors. But they do not like to spend more salary or wage expenditure to employ full time extra labors, instead of increasing extra abnormal working hours to current labors to achieve productivity of raising, due to the cost will be increased if they choose to employ extra full time labors if they want to raise productivity. However, I feel they will raise productivity in the short term, but they will not raise productivity in the long term when they choose to raise their current labors abnormal working hours per working day.

The assumption will be made regarding to the relationship between the HK labor market's abnormal long time working hours factor and whether it can influence Hong Kong economic growth in long time for this research economic problem. For example, how many hours Hong Kong labor would actually work or how much workers have efficient productivity and efficiency and how much salaries or wages would be affected as a result of the increasing in working time(hours) in Hong Kong employment market.

I shall apply endogenous growth theory to Hong Kong labor market. As this theory indicates that this model also incorporated a new concept of human capital, whose capital is increasing rates of return. Research done in this area has focused on what increases human capital (e.g. education) or technological change (e.g. innovation) to influence HK economic growth. In macro economic environment, it indicates that economic growth means the increase in the market value of the products and services produced by the country's economy over time. It is conventionally measured as the percent rate of increase in real growth domestic product or real GDP. The growth of the ratio of GDP to population (GDP per capital, per capita income). Thus, an increase in growth is caused by more efficient use of inputs is referred to as intensive growth. GDP growth is caused only be increased in such as capital, population or territory is called extensive growth. Thus, in economy growth theory, typically refers growth off potential output, i.e. production is at full employment. However, HK unemployment ratio is still high to compare other developed or developing countries, although the labors supply are enough to HK employment market.

The working time is the period of time that an individual spends at paid occupation labor. Many countries regulate the work week by law, such as minimum daily rest periods, annual holidays and a maximum number of working hours per week. Working time may vary from person to person often depending on location, cultural, lifestyle choice and the profitability of the individual's livelihood.

Generally, most Hong Kong employers need labors work long time working hours abnormally. For example, low educational workers, such as security occupations of labors need to work per working day is twelve hours or more, restaurant waiters and dish cleaners also need to work ten to twelve hours or more per working day, bank counter cashiers or audit firm staffs also need to work over time from 10 to 12 hours or more per working day and who have no extra salaries for over time salaries payment commonly. Standard working hours or normal working hours refers to the legislation to limit the working hours per day, per week, per month or per year. If an employee needs to work overtime, the employer will need to pay overtime payments to employees as required in the law. Generally speaking, standard working hours countries word wide are around 40 to 44 hours per week (but not everywhere: such as France employers need labors work from 35 hours per week, North Korea employers need labors work up to 112 hours per week). Maximum working hours refers that the employee can't work than the level specified in the maximum working hours law. It seems that Hong Kong many employers had needed labors to work above standard working hours per week to compare to other developed countries, e.g. America, France, England, New Zealand etc. developed countries.

In conclusion, in my viewpoint, HK employers need to provide on job training to current labors to aim to raise their efficiency to productivity in the long time. Because when their labors had been trained to let them to learn how to use special skill to finish their job duties easily, then they will not need to spend much time (additional working hours) to finish their job duties per working day. On the one hand, HK employers need to measure to compare what benefits are in favor of standard working hours to whose employees. The benefits include, such as promoting work life balance and enjoy family life, increasing time for leisure and rest, beneficial to health and employees can have more time to pursue further studies as well as employers do not need to pay higher salaries to longer working hours employees or overtime pay boost income as most HK companies pay time and a half to some employees only. On the other hand, HK employers need to measure to compare what benefits are against standard working hours to employers, such as employing many part time working hours employees to assist normal working hours full time employees rather than needing full time employees work abnormal hours daily, lowering or cancelling year and bonus etc. Moreover, HK employers may also use various measure to offset the increased cost of running businesses, such as lowering average hourly annual compensation. However, when HK employees are forced to work part time jobs, who may need to acquire additional employment to maintain their standard living. Even, HK employers only force employees to work overtime in some situations. Appropriate standard working hours can vary across different industries based on the type of work performed. Such as some HK certain professional positions are difficult to define in terms of appropriate working hours. Issues can arise with employers expecting employees to work extra hours "off the clock" in order to keep costs down. Thus, I believe that HK labors abnormal working hours time issue ought be decreased and HK employers ought employ extra workers assistance to share current labors' workload to help them to raise productivity and efficiency and HK economy will grow fast in the long time. Finally, my research aims to find that the number of hours worked is a more responsive measure of the state of the labor market than employment in HK. Comparing the number of hours worked to indicators of the wider economy shows that it is likely to be demand from HK firms (employers) which is driving the numbers of hours, rather than individual job applicant supply to HK employment market. My analysis also show that the HK appears to have developed a long working hours culture to compare other developed countries, such as America, England, Canada etc. In fact, in the presence of HK firms may even invest to find which are more profitable to able to reduce their every employee's abnormal working hours daily rather than normal number of working hours of their every employee.

Finally, I shall recommend some methods to rise the living standard to low income level households group in any countries. On the income policy, I recommend governments ought implement the progressive tax policy, so the income taxes tend to be progressive to the middle and high income level of households. It aims to achieve the low income level group and the middle and high income level groups whose income level to be balanced. Whereas taxes on payroll and consumption usually are regressive, due to payroll and consumption taxes are more useful than income taxes for increasing revenues taxes on income and payroll are the least conductive to economic growth, so payroll taxes can raise growth of employment in possible. Because the low income level of households have no more effort to spend to buy any expensive products or foods generally, so who can pay less taxes when who spend less. Otherwise, because the middle or high income levels of households have more effort to spend to buy any expensive products or foods generally, so who need pay more taxes when who spend more. It is possible to reduce the level amount of difference of savings between the low income level of households and the middle income level of households. Finally, I conclude that the method of taxes on payroll and consumption usually are regressive and the method of income taxes tend to be progressive to the middle and high income level of households, which are possible to raise the low income level of households of living standard for long term if governments could attempt to achieve these two policies to apply to the low income level group and the middle income level groups both, such as income tax and payroll or consumption tax policies both. It aims to raise the better of standard of life to the low income level household and to assist the low income level household can be upgrade to the middle income level household group in the short time quickly.

Economists claim to be scientists or technicians who study fact, not values, who make scientific studies and predictions to decide why this matter is caused and to find the reasons. Often the public sector economists in USA predict the economic processes and find the facts of the world have not supported the economists‘ models wrongly. However, economists have ethical rules to control their behaviors to be judged any matter and to give the corrective and reasonable decisions to let public to know correctively. Hence, who can't attempt to mislead facts to present to let public to receive the wrongly message to achieve themselves unreasonable benefits and rewards. In fact, economist is similar to lawyer or accountant profession, who need to provide a "service" discipline to give corrective and reasonable judgement and facts and who can not attempt to mislead to publish whose economic research reports to let public to get wrong information frequently. I believe that the scientific of economics of the 20th century fully accepts the ethical separation. Economic theory is seen as a positive science which has to analyze and to explain the mechanisms of economic processes. Ethical valuations should not form part of the economist's research program. Modern economics stresses rational calculation, the base material objections and scientific neutrality on moral issues. I think whose idea is concerned micro economy is based on assumptions of rationally selfish behavior.

Whether what is concerned to current ethical crisis in economics? Economic matters have been debated throughout human history. I feel economic ethical matters which can be concerned in aspects, such as wealth accumulation, lending, business and commerce economic issues, journals or reports or books publishing. Due to any economic matters happen in economic processes which will be recorded in history, then economists will analyze why these issues are caused and find what reasons which cause the economic issue happening is discussed by theology, ethics and politics issues are as view points. So, the moral and ethics is needed to concern to any economists when who need to do any economic research nowadays.

Economy is concerned to human will face limited resources to use or spend, so economy theory indicates to be researched what methods how human chooses to allocate resources to achieve the efficient and effective result. Economy aims to achieve human rationality to control the desire to acquire material products in order to allow better satisfaction of the true human need. Many economists concern for others now directly affects one's own welfare and commitment drives between personal choice and personal welfare and thus undermines modern economics ethic. Individuals frequently display commitment, acting against their own welfare in favor of the group. This element of ethical behavior has been ignored by economists and needs to be brought into the analysis. Although ethical motivation are relevant to economists, but the capabilities approach is more concerned with social achievement. To a large degree, this is a theory of distributive justice that economy and political science and philosophy theories which have more relationship among of these three subjects theories.

Why ethic relates to labor behavior

I shall give some current economists' judgement to indicate how well human are doing according to the capability standard to prove why employers need to concern moral behavior. The capability approaching requires that many means be provided to every person. This is an alternative to social achievement from economics approach, which uses the quantity of commodities available for consumption. The conventional measure of the standard of living (GDP/ head) has been subject to sustained criticism in recent times, one source of the complaints is the capability theorists. This capabilities approach is a new inter-disciplinary social science and there are still many problems with this approach to concern ethical issues of mainstream economics. However, some economists feel that ethical motivations exist and play a role in human's actual behavior. Human well being refers to living a full human life. It measures to show the things that demonstrate a good life being lived. So, human functioning achievements, must be the focus. Possession of a certain quantity of commodities, however, may be necessary in order to achieve human functioning. This provides social success in delivering well being across our society. Moreover, some scientists who also believe the standard of social success may be limited to basic functioning. Alternatively, a rich of human group may be accepted, but social success may be considered for only a small proportion of the population. So, for each theorist, we need to ask these following questions. Does the theorist present an ethical view of motivation? Does the theorist adopt a deep mind of human well being? In the assessment of social success, does the theorist concern human functioning achievements and means to promote functioning achievements?

I shall analyze on individual psychology, household psychology and social achievement three aspects to indicate labor morality and raising productivity and even economic growth has close relationship as below:

In economic view, household means a family which has female control functioning. On the individual and public policy means that support individual achievements. However, in concept analysis, I shall indicate three levels of analysis to economic ethic of human behavior. The lowest level is individual, it is individual psychology, human functioning and ethical motivation. The middle level is household, it is household management, moral education, character formation. The highest level is the city, it is social achievement (Public policy supports equipment needs for individual capability achievement and formative law). So, human's behavioral is an assumption of modern economics. From history viewpoint, our economic conditions are largely agricultural with some mining, manufacturing and commerce, there was limited scope for domestic and international markets; mutual give and take, lending and borrowing between households was widespread. Commonly, these activities are general human economic behavior of reasons to cause these business activities in our society.

Firstly, on individual psychology aspect, human's economy of behavior is in our society, human needs do this economy behavior because human needs have good life and education, the good life required leisure and the good use of leisure time to do leisure activities with friends. Otherwise, leisure required freedom from the duties of earning a living. It was commonly accepted that the good life is required to work to earn, such as labors, traders, professions, farmers etc. service or labor occupations their individual behavior is aim to achieve earning for good life and education. So, who need to spend some time to do economic activities to aim to earn some time for leisure and education.

Secondly, on household management psychology aspect, in general, managing revenues and expenditures is a part of household management. However, household management requires moderation on the desires for food, wine, sex and sleep. So, in labor economy relationship, household seems to be the frame of mind and habits needed for engineering to make sense. In old age, expenditure on subsistence continues, but no one will pay for the labor of the old. Saving for old age, therefore is sensible. However, if one is habituated in youth to lazy, one will find it hand to change later. Nevertheless, these habits are unsustainable in old age, when one can't be labor and generate income. Hence, in labor economy view, moderation is an essential element of good household management. Although, wealth is also important, but more important is the knowledge or skill of household management. However, if one has no leisure and is unable to develop his capabilities (including bodily and non-bodily pleasures to easy to live with). Then, productivity will be reduce and inefficient work, due to the labor is hard to work, who feel himself/herself is such as a machine and who has no much time to rest often. Also the earning of friendship is also important, including certain market relationships in our modern societies. Clearly human's labor economy of behavior of household management in the broad sense is a comprehensive act and part of a way of human life. Hence, an ethical understanding is also needed, such as friendship relationship to complete household management in the middle level of household management between the city level and individual level. On functioning achievement and freedom to individual of labor economy behavior, it includes education, increased physical training etc. economic benefits to our individual in our society. Just as the city is a complex structure, so is human psychology to cause labor economy behavior. Justice in the city is defined as each class (and each individual within the class) doing its own job, justice in the individual is defined as each part of individual doing its own job. Hence, a good city has all of the individuals correctly assigned to the different classes and each individual and each class performs its appropriate job. Similarly, the good individual has each of labor's performing its job appropriately.

In the final social achievement aspect, it concerns micro. As the growth of the healthy city showed up to a certain point, economic development is required in terms of the city's physical size and population. So, modern economic principles are adopted (such as economic development and the division of labor). Nevertheless, our society must be justify to some degree to market relations. Various property rights and exchange justice must be enforced. These principles, however are limited by other ethical principles guiding the laws. Nevertheless, citizens are to be banned from engaging in most occupations. For example, the moral dangers of commercial activities are great. Moreover, market are limited to a specific location and regulated by market regulators. Although, duties are not imposed on foreign trade, prohibitions apply to various unnecessary imports and to exports of necessities. Hence, it will influence labor demand and job supply to influence the country's economic development in any time. To analyze labor economy, we need to know human nature and to establish the functions of human beings. These functions are shared with human beings, e.g. humans need to eat, drink. As a general rule, the passions that drive human to satisfy these needs, but it is of limited amount to supply. So, these factors will influence labor's behavior between action, motivation and character. However, every organization is influenced to economic growth every year by its staff individual behavior, such as its staff individual has passions and emotions disposed toward bad action and decides to act well for other reasons, e.g. the staff feels fear of detection or punishment and then who will act well because of the staff's self control to avoid the firm will dismiss him/her in the firm. It seems the staff's passion, emotion will influence whose behavior to be good or bad to do whose work in whose firm. Hence, the firm needs have economic analysis to decide to dismiss the staff or not dismiss the staff if it discovered whose behavior is not acceptable to its firm and what it will be influenced from whose bad behavior in the short term and long term. If the staff is very important and if who left this firm, this firm will face business failure challenge because it has no any right applicant or another staff who can do this staff's job easily. Hence, in labor economy analysis, the firm needs to judge the benefits are much or the losses are much before which decide to dismiss the staff.

What are ethics? Ethics are a set of values or group of moral principles that are right and good a code or principles of behavior or conduct governing an individual or group. For example, when a engineer needs to do any researching jobs which concern to engineering, who needs to increase whose ability as engineer to responsibly confront moral issues raised by technological activity, not always in short term best interest, and long term into decision making ethics are imprecise, complex, and in a given situation may conflict. Who will have these questions to concern before who does his duties, such as does it pass the benefits /harm test? Whom does it harm? Whom does it benefit? Can these be justified, cost/ benefit analysis risk assessment? Does it treat everyone equally? equitable? If not, can the differences be justified? However, any employer needs to concern whose labor ethics issues, who have four aspects need to be considered, such as: On the first concerning aspect, it is working condition ethics, whether the employer's act is moral right when it respects right relevant to a work environment or employment condition of situation. For example, whether the employer can provide whose employees have rights for life, liberty, pursuit of happiness, human rights and non-human rights, e.g. clean and safe working environment or fair salary and welfare, unreasonable normal working hours. On the second concerning aspect, it is duty ethics, whether the employer acts it is right when it conforms with ethics duties to whose employees, e.g. uphold promise, be fair treatment to job nature and duty, respect personal freedom, duty to protect the weak, duty to comply with employment laws, duty to do job to best of ability. On the third concerning aspect, it is utilitarianism ethic, whether the employer has right action consists in producing good consequences to whose employees, e.g. good intentions, outcomes, honesty, fairness, conscientiousness etc. On the final concerning aspect, it is the situational ethics, which means that depending on the specific circumstance, different rights, duties, values, etc. the right circumstance may be applied to whose labors, e.g. whether the workers work in the dirty and dark factory and who need to work abnormal working hours. It seems that if the working environment is not suitable to the employees to feel to work, it will influence the labors raise to work inefficient and poor performance.

So, employers need to concern their ethics to labor, it include moral development to labor, which are often classified such as, obedience or punishment, marketplace morality, conformity, law and order, social contract, universal human rights and integrity whole environment ethic moral development of issues. However, emotion is one important factor to influence labor's individual performance and productivity and efficiency to any employer. How emotional labor and ethic of care will influence productivity. Employers concern care which ought be more than labor itself. Labor's activity that is fundamentally about maintaining, continuing and repairing the working economic world, so that labor can live in it as well as possible. An ethic of labor care is more than a list of moral principles, the ethic of care labor elements, it includes attentiveness, responsibility, competence and responsiveness. However, employers need to make distinctions between " caring for" and "caring about" to labor ethic. "Caring about" is directed toward less concrete objects/subjects. It is a general form of commitment to employees, when "caring for" focuses on a specific object/subject and responds to the particular, physical, spiritual, intellectual and emotional needs of labor. Caring labor is too inclusive of all kinds of economic activities. So employers ought not care relations too narrowly, but should include care is given by extended to employees‘ families, such as domestic workers and workers in hospitals and teachers etc. service labor occupations. So, labor care ethic relates to the work that employers do under the working conditions within which the employers' labor. Also, a labor care ethic is a deeply relational framework involving both labor care activities and practices as well as a habit of labor care mind. So, employers ought presume that dependent is valued, accepted and universal, it necessitates that care labor to every is shared equally and the society policy also needs to be promoted care labor values to let employers to concern this care labor issue. Care ethic means that empathy and responsiveness, among others, coming out of practices and experiences of " doing care". However, the important aspects of a care ethic that complicates our understanding of the reproduction of alienated labor under capitalism as well as in carrying out care labor, caring for the recipient is an expected part of that work.

In labour ethic view, employers ought attempt to answer

this question. Does the expectation of such affective emotions necessitate a different formulation of compensation? In examining the relationship between an ethic of care and the alienation under capitalist relations of production. For example: What does make a "good work" ? Is a good worker someone who cares about whose work? How much should the worker care for the recipient of the labour? What does about the customer service representative who care about assisting someone? or does the retail salesperson care about helping someone look good? or does the carpenter care for the wood with which he is working? Whether the worker may or may not take time, be attentive, responsive and responsible. So, I suggest "caring about" and "caring for" the work and the recipient implies a relational experience with others. Many workers care about the outcome of their labour, whether a final product or service. They take pride in their work, they care about doing a good job, they take care of the people with whom who encounter in the process. In this way, workers make their work meaningful, who attempt to connect to it and to those who are "served" when carrying out the work.

Nowadays, human are encountering of an expended service economy, care and the emotional labour involved in such work. For example, luxury hotel workers are interactive service workers both consented to activity investing in the work, also luxury service is not only about what workers do; it is also about how they do it. Luxury service means that how workers make their jobs meaningful, become invested in them, and construct images of themselves as skilled and autonomous. For example, flight attendants who are the caring and emotional labour that is expected of these workers and it is the caring for the recipient, which allows workers to find meaning, creativity and feel connected to the work itself. I also think that labouring makes "real" something outside of the individual, the commodity as value is imposed external to the thing and to the labour itself. Under conditions of private property, the worker is disconnected from whose own creative powers and the objects of the labour become alien to the worker. So, I think employers ought not take away any labour whose individual's specific life, e.g. For long term abnormal working hours will reduce any labour's leisure and family private time.

However, I think labour can divide two kinds of physical labour and emotional labour. For example, the a factory worker works from whose own body and so who is a physical labour. Otherwise, a flight attendant works from whose own feelings and so who is a emotional labour. However, for the particular features of service -oriented labour, who needs to take "caring for" someone is central, necessarily alter these survival techniques. In care work, it is the consumers/recipients of care who expect that those who do caring work care about the work who do and care for the recipients of their care labour, e.g. hotel employees need to shoe genuine care and concern for guests' needs. So, care is the expected and central element of the labour and I think that health attendants and nurses home health carers etc. service workers who need provide more emotional service to whose clients, so who belong to emotional service labour seriously. For example, nursing profession, nurses are thought about as caring, moral creatures who show kindness and comfort to their patients. It is the doctors who are assumed to possess skills and knowledge. How care labour may be negatively affected, such as underpaid, overworked may happen in a situation where the care-giver is compensated unjustly and treated unfairly. Is it possible to argue that if care labour or any labour carried out in the context of a care ethic, the work that is done could be so much better for the whole of society and for the person doing the work and recipients of the work? In an ethic of care that predominates, would we simply value the labour of chid-care workers or home care attendants etc. workers? Would we reflect better compensation, better treatment and better working conditions because our relationship with ourselves and each other are acknowledged and values? Hence, care activities are needed to focus on caring labour, e.g. nurses, personal attendants or home care workers and child care workers. That is, assuming the existence of a care ethic, such questions must be applied to any and all work activities that we do. Does every economic activity contain caring practices, even traditionally non care labour? I think caring about what we do and how we do it, we may help to improve our relations with others, thus reflecting an ethic of care. Does caring labour help to make invisible, reduce its harm to the self and society? It may be true that workers cared for their work, product or service, this would serve the needs of the employers quite well. How do we care for/about something but against the exploitation produced by capital labour relations? Is it good for society as a whole to care about what you do, care for the work you do, Does the product you make or the service you provide even if it enriches the owner and exploits the worker? What about the office cleaner who cleans the office effectively and efficiently in order to keep whose job that who desperately needs. Should the office cleaner care about doing a good job, care for the faceless people who doesn't know?

A care ethic both encourages this type of work ethic and at the same time, these relations are created and who serve are expected to care for and about the recipients of care, the customer is always right. However, structural inequalities between consumers and workers are normalized in the process. For the nurses and home care workers, the work becomes their own, who become attached to the work, connected to the process and the final outcome, and the work gives meaning to their live. At the same time, when workers don't care about whose work, when they don't care for their charges, or for the service who are offering. Should it, when may the labour be a child care provider neglecting the needs of the child? Or of the overworked social worker dismissing the needs of whose client in order to fill paperwork that who is directed to complete. Hence, I recommend employers need to concern about care is needed such as a practice, value, ethic activity to their labours. The elements of care, its affective emotional and relational qualities help to give meaning to the work for the worker. At the same time, it could be an ethic of care, where individuals view themselves as relational, identifying our connections to others and mutual responsibilities for each other become the necessary conditions for a working class politics.

Labour market equilibrium is an important issue to be concerned in law economy and ethic aspect. Workers prefer to work when the wage is high, and firms prefer to hire when the wage is low generally. Labour market equilibrium "balance out" the conflicting desires of workers and firms and determines the wage and employment observed in the labour market. If labour markets are competitive and if firms and workers are free to enter and leave; the equilibrium allocation of workers to firms is efficient; the sorting of workers and firms are accumulated by trading each other. In fact, labour markets are efficient plays a role by the public policy. Many government programs are often debated whether the particular policy leads to a more efficient allocation of resources or whether the efficiency costs are substantial. Labour market equilibrium occurs when labour supply equals labour demand, generating the competitive wage(w) and employment (E). The wage (w) is the market clearing wage because any other wage level would create either upward or downward pressures on the wage. It would be too many jobs to supply, but the few available workers or too many workers competing for the few available job determined. Due to the competitive wage level is determined in this industry fashion, each firm in the industry hires workers up to the point where the value of marginal product of labour equals the competitive wage. Then, it seems the industry worker's wage level has arrived the maximum labour market wage level. So, employers ought not need to increase whose wage to attract more workers to choose to do whose industry often because it is not reasonable wage level increasing when the labour supply number is enough at the moment. Also the labour market of the industry has implied it's worker demand numbers has arrived the equal level of job supply numbers in the stage. What is caused to happen by worker surplus? When the difference between what the worker receives, that is the competitive wage(w) and the value of the worker's time outside the labour market gives the gains to workers. So, it will cause the excess workers have a value of marginal product that is less than their value of time. In effect, those workers are not being efficiently used by the labour market. So, firms ought to learn how to allocate the right number of persons to different positions that maximizes the total gains and firms ought need to learn how to form trade in the labour market in any efficient allocation way.

Search of labour economy, the central aim is to examine how a work perspective, countries can develop their skills base to increase both the quantity and the productivity of labour employed in the country. Inadequate education and skills of labour development can influence any countries' overall economic development in long term. So, governments need to achieve good policies to solve this issue. Due to skills and education development is central to improve productivity. Because productivity is an important source of improved living standards and growth. Other critical factors include macroeconomic policies maximize opportunities for poor employment growth, an enabling environment is for enterprise development and fundamental investments in education, health and physical to income level households. So, effective skills development systems which is needed to connect education to technical training, technical training to labour market entry and labour market entry to workplace to long life learning to concentrate on providing to low income level households.

Productivity growth can reduce production costs and increase returns on investments. Some of which provide greater income for business owners which some are given higher wages to labours. However, the productivity of individuals may be reflected in employment rates, wage rates, stability of employment, job satisfaction or employability across jobs or industries. The productivity of enterprises, in addition to output per worker may measure in terms of market share and export performance. The benefits to societies from higher individual and enterprise productivity may be evident in increased competitiveness and employment or in a shift of employment from low to higher productivity sector. So, employers can use this method to measure every employee's morality and job behaviour performance to judge whether their job ethic and job attitude whether which can adopt to continue to work in whose organizational environment. If the employer discovered the employee's morality and job behaviour performance and job attitude is not achieved to whose work performance standard, then who can decide to either reduce whose salary or dismiss him/her or not increasing whose salary for long term any decision. So, labour ethic issue is very important to influence economic growth to any countries.

Whether labour ethic has close relationship to economic growth. I feel this issues concerns any stage of the labour life cycle and organization life cycles, it includes the link between the design of economic theory and labour individual morality and job behaviour and performance. In fact, we need to suppose all research questions and labour economy is as mapping to particular stages of an individual's life cycle to labour economy ought be related to the accumulation of human (labour) capital, labour market entry and labour supply choices, behaviour within firms and household decision making. Prior years some researchers had been carrying on observing experiments to the women and men labour work and in whose nature environment for weeks, and then used various treatments, including manipulating the environment in such a way to increase and decrease rest periods. They got result long time working hours and not rest time, it will reduce labours(workers) of productivity. So, it implies the overall productivity and individual productivity will be reduced. Although, the employers have enough workers to work in the natural working environment at the same time, but due to who have no enough rest time to provide to them, then their workers' working performance and efficiency will be fallen. Nowadays, industrialized countries had began to consider how to plan similar welfare reforms, researching the economic reasons and consequences to labour economic issue, such as United States, the United King, Sweden and Germany, it seems economic growth and law ethic has close relationship. However, labour economy includes how to measure labour's emotion to raise productivity, as well as how technological change, education, employment and wages which can assist labour to raise productivity. Due to good labour emotion and labour ethic can raise productivity, then raising productivity can also raise economic growth finally. So, I believe which have close cause and effect relationship.

However, many economists have long been pessimistic that an experimental approach could offer such illustrations of labour ethic and economic growth of cause and effect relationship in their field. Who feel labour bad emotion or bad labour ethic has no any influence to economic growth. In fact, the economic world is extremely complicated, so human needs to have economic laws is set by controlled experiment to measure or judge whether labour ethic and economic growth which has or has no any close relationship. If economists have no such test, economic laws, who can't perform such as the controlled experiments of chemists or biologists very well because who can't easily control other important factors to observe why labour emotion or ethic has reason to influence overall economic growth to any country if they neglect to carry on researching experiment between the relationship of ethic and productivity and economic growth. So I recommend economists need have participants in the natural field experiment to carry on researching to any labour emotion or ethic issue to gather statistic information of population to get prediction more accurately if who want to measure whether labour emotion or ethic and productivity which has close relationship to any country's economic growth for long term.

Why employers need to concern
ethic to decide whether outsourcing is suitable to raise productivity growth to their businesses

Generally, outsourcing can be defined as an organization is entering into a contract with another organization to operate and manage one or more of its business processes. Due to employers face increasing competitive pressure to remain focused, flexible, cost competitive and competent, so outsourcing can access to low cost specialized talent. However, outsourcing means the contracting out of a employer's non core, non efficient, non revenue producing activities to specialists. It is a strategic management tool, such as restructure or contracting out to third party to carry out certain functions efficiently. The most common types of outsourcing are manufacturing outsourcing, information technology outsourcing and business process outsourcing (including processes related to accounting, human resources, benefits, payroll and finance etc. aspects). In fact, employers decide outsourcing reasons which include such as: market pressure to be price competitive, availability of cheap labour elsewhere, abundance of highly talented skilled labour in themselves country, pressure is from investing to cut cost, increase profit and show growth, focusing on core business operations and expanding global presence etc. factors. Many employers begin to concern the ethical and moral implication of outsourcing issue to cause the political and business discussion nowadays. Also, many economists have for-or-against social debates for outsourcing ethic issue. However, outsourcing can bring these benefits to some businesses. For example, if a car can be made more cheaper in China, it should be; if a telephone enquiry can be processed more cheaper in any Asia country, it should be. All such transactions raise real incomes on both sides as resources are advantageously redeployed, with added investment and growth in the exporting country, and lower prices in the importing country.

However, conservative economists argue that the sole mission of a corporation is to maximize profit for the benefits of shareholders. They also contend that in a global economy, outsourcing does not mean net job loss. They argue that more jobs will be created global since the cost labour lowered. The term "global" comes to mind when discussing today's large Corporations. It is hard to say which locally a company belongs to. In fact, outsourcing can also cause disadvantages. Sudden loss of jobs and loss of income can lead to economic depression in smaller regions. As the biggest employer in a those towns/cities closes down factories and start manufacturing in Asia or outsource the manufacturing altogether to a foreign this party. So, the country will raise unemployment rate suddenly when local jobs are outsourced to overseas.

Morality of local employees in favor of outsourcing hiring low wage employees elsewhere is another point of contention of this debate. The (capitalist) economy based on the law of supply and demand. In such economy, allocation or resources, including capital and labour is generally determined by market forces. Therefore, it is reasonable and expectable that companies would seek the best option available to employ their capital and recruit in a global economy. Due to it is assumed that local responsibility has less meaning when the economy and company operate globally. So, it causes any country employers don't concern labour ethic issue after outsourcing influences to its local labour. Nowadays, many employers would agree that the acts of downsizing/outsourcing for pure financial reasons (i.e. choosing short-term investor gain over employee welfare) are very often morally wrong. However, without clear morally relevant distinction (either in academia or business press) between a company's priority to the shareholder and that to its workers, it is very hard defend that position. This is justified because shareholders have taken a risk in placing their money in the hands of the corporation, and are thereby due compensation. Shareholders can potentially lose something who have placed into the corporation. However, workers have placed something at risk when accepting a job, they lose future potential earnings due to corporate outsourcing. At the very least, the worker has foregone other possible job opportunities. Even more importantly, many workers have invested in their houses, their local communities and in their lifestyle with the expectation of a steady income. When the worker's investment in a corporation is not of the same sort as the shareholder's, it constitutes a risk nevertheless, and so the worker's position is not different to that of the shareholder. However, I believe that evaluating the differences of that risk will depend upon of each individual's relationship with the company and their personal values. For example, CEO pay is a completely separate issue on its own. It is a very popular subject in current academic and business press. Even if it is different subject, it has moral implications in regards to outsourcing.

In general, CEO can earn a more percent raise to compare to regular worker's percent raise. In common, companies show the reason of CEO percent raise more is that there is enough causation to conclude that outsourcing contributes to profitability / stock price increase of a company, this the rise in CEO compensation. The ethic issue here is that, if the market rewards a company for improving it is bottom line or for cutting costs why is it ethically wrong for a company to outsource at the expense of local labour force. After all, the reason for an existence of company is to provide value to its shareholders. However, I think CEOs aims to achieve themselves benefits, who may improve their bottom line when hurting workers and communities. The morality of further rewarding CEO's who knowingly undertook layoffs of his employees in favor of outsourcing their work to a third party or move those jobs to a low wage country is very troubling.

In fact, outsourcing raises many concerns for working professional for and communities. It has long held personal and community values, such as , loyalty and commitment to employees. However, as much as economic prosperity global trade can bring, if does bring devastation as well. Availability of cheap products is appreciable, but you need to have a job and a income to consume those products. For many, outsourcing hurts at the heart of their livelihoods. Also, I argue to against outsourcing is that growing concern of issues of privacy related to outsourcing information creates an ethical and legal issue. The concern is against outsourcing (in specific cases of Accounting, Human Resource and Medical outsourcing) because of the fear of sensitive information's safety and confidentiality. So, employers ought check references and transcripts and perform background checks to minimize the risk of hiring someone who lacks ethic or morality to do whose outsourcing job duties. Moreover, outsourcing firms may indicate that all of their employees are highly educated, trained professionals of the highest honesty. Finally, I recommend employers ought to consider these questions before who decide to outsource, such as: does stockholders welfare out weight that of a company's employees? Is profit maximization ethical? Is it ethical to reward the upper management for cutting cost by eliminating jobs? Should the compensation for upper management with held if the profit is achieved by outsourcing? Is it ethical to reward a management that repeatedly shown disregard to its employees? (increasing workload, constant layoff, choosing the cheapest labour over quality). Is it right for the public to expect a company to keep all its employment locally, (at a higher cost) but at the same time sell products at comparable rate with foreign companies who use cheap labour? Does a company ethically bound a provide maximum occupation in its home country? Does it have a duty to its local community? In case of outsourcing is the employer ethically bound to retrain the employees? So, all these questions are very important concerning outsourcing influence, if every employer can concern these questions, then who can decide whose outsourcing reason is right or wrong more clearly. To conclude, any employer ought need to decide whether outsourcing is the best of one method to raise productivity for long term strategic plan.

How labour morality can reduce poverty in society

In conclusion, I shall use labour morality can assist society to reduce poverty. In labour economy view, a livelihood comprises the capabilities of assets (including both material and social resources) and activities required for a means of living. A livelihood is sustainable when it can cope with and recover from shocks, maintain or enhance its capabilities and asset, when not undermining the natural resource base. It has three elements: livelihood resources, livelihood strategies and institutional processes and organizational structures. So, I think that productivity will raise, even poverty and crime will be also reduced, due to the low income level householder family which can be upgraded to increase whose income level and quality of living standard to the middle income level householder family. When governments can promote the labour morality to which employers to let them to know labour morality and productivity has close relationship.

How to understand the complex and differentiated process through which livelihoods are constructed, governments need to analyse which countries themselves local citizen to let their knowledge, perceptions and interests be heard. There are three insights into poverty. The first is the realization that when economic growth may be essential for poverty reduction, there is not an automatic an automatic relationship between the two since if all depends on the capabilities of the poor to take advantage of expanding economic opportunities. Secondly, there is the realization that poverty as conceived by the poor themselves. It is not just a question of low income, but also includes other factors, such as bad health, illiteracy, lack of social services etc. Finally, it is now often know their situation and need best and must therefore be involved in the design of policies and project intended to better their lot. So, governments and employers need to identify those issues of subjects areas for effective poverty reduction, either at the local level or at the policy level. This is in principle on open-ended process, certain emphasis is given to the introduction of improved technologies as well as social and economic investments to every country's government. The three fundamental attributes to any developing countries or developed countries themselves countries if which plan to raise economic growth and to reduce poverty to upgrade or low income level householders to rise to the middle income level householder family. The three attributes include the possession of human capabilities, such as education, skills, health, psychological orientation; access to tangible and intangible assets and the existence of economic activities. However, a livelihood comprises the capabilities, assets, including both material and social resources and activities required for a means of living. A livelihood is sustainable when it can cope with and recover from stresses and shocks and maintain or enhance its capabilities and assets both now and in the future. To solve poverty problem, it includes not only physical and natural resources, but also every country's social and human capital issues. Every country's government also needs to facilitate an understanding of the causes of poverty by focusing on the variety of factors at different levels that directly or indirectly determine or constrain low income level householder's access to and assets of different kinds. Also every country's government needs to assess the direct and indirect effects on low income level householder's living conditions then, for example one dimensional productivity or income criteria.

Over the various components of a livelihood, the most complex is the portfolio of assets out of which people construct their living. This portfolio includes tangible assets, such as stores, e.g. food stocks, stores of value, such as gold, jewelry, cash saving and resources, e.g. land, water, trees, live stocks farm, equipment as well as intangible assets, such as claims, for example, demands and appeals which can be made be material, moral or other practical support and access, which is the opportunity to practice to use a resource, store or service or to obtain information, material, technology, employment, food or income. Hence, if employers can provide enough capital input to make whose labours feel fairness, satisfactory and reasonable working environment and compensation. I believe that these satisfactory demand of labours who can raise productivity to their employers more easily. In labour economic view, any employers, governments or companies organizational resources inputs can divide four kinds of capital nature. Firstly, the natural capital is natural resources stocks, e.g. soil, water, air, genetic resources etc. and environmental services, e.g. hydrological cycle, pollution sinks, etc. from which resources flows and services useful for livelihoods are derived . Secondly, economic or financial capital is the capital base, e.g. cash , credit/debt, savings and other economic assets, including basic infrastructure and production equipment and technologies which are essential for the pursuit of and livelihood strategy. Thirdly, human capital is the skill, knowledge, ability to labour and good health and physical capability important for the successful pursuit of different livelihood strategies and finally, social capital is the social resources, e.g. networks, social claims, social relations, which people draw when pursuit different livelihood strategies, requiring co-ordinated action. So, any country or employee which has a plan to know how to allocate which resources efficiently, it will raise productivity and economic growth and poverty reducing more easily. So, it seems labour morality can raise productivity which has close relationship to any employer, even labour morality and economic growth which has close relationship to any country. So, any country and any employer which ought not neglect labour morality for long term.

TWO

THE HISTORICAL DEVELOPMENT OF BEHAVIORAL ECONOMICS AND FUNCTION

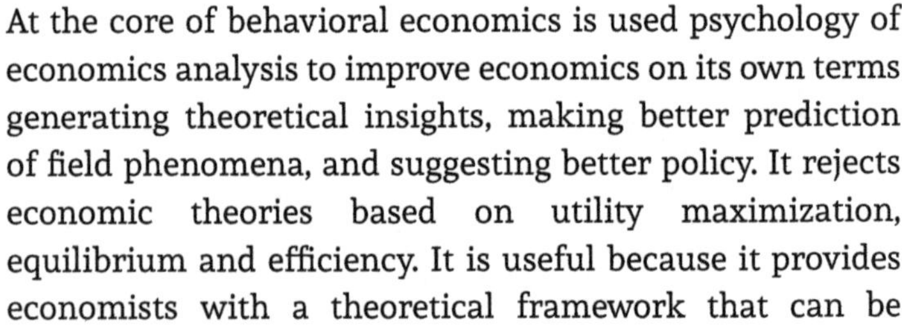

At the core of behavioral economics is used psychology of economics analysis to improve economics on its own terms generating theoretical insights, making better prediction of field phenomena, and suggesting better policy. It rejects economic theories based on utility maximization, equilibrium and efficiency. It is useful because it provides economists with a theoretical framework that can be applied to almost any form of economic (and even non-economic) behavior.

Simplifying much assumption that are not central to the economic theory. For example, there is nothing in core theory that specifies that people should not care about fairness, that they should weight risky outcomes in a linear fashion, or that they must discount the future at a constant rate. Other assumption simply acknowledge human limits on computational power and self-interest. These assumptions can be considered procedurally rational because human needs to solve problems that are often so complex that who can't be solved exactly by even modern computer technology.

Theories in behavioral economics should be judged by reality, generality and tractability concepts. We share the positivist view that the ultimate test of a theory is the accuracy of its predictions. But we also believe that better predictions are likely to result from theories with more realistic assumptions. In psychology, such as connectionist models that capture some of the essential features of neural functioning, which are based on utility maximization, yet are reaching the point where they are able to predict many judgement and behavioral phenomena. Contrary to the positivistic view, however, we believe that predictions of feelings (e.g., of subjective well-being) should be an important goal.

Most of the ideas in behavioral economics are not new. When economics first became identified as a distinct field of study, psychology didn't exist as a discipline. For example, "invisible hand" and "the wealth of Nations" which belong to theory to moral sentiments, which laid out psychological principles of individual behavior that are arguably as profound as whose economic observations. Another example, such as a simple model of social utility means that one person's utility was affected by another person's payoff. However, the rejection of academic psychology by economists, which constructed an account of economic behavior built up from assumptions about the

nature-that is, the psychology of homo-economics. Nowadays, economists hoped their discipline could be like a natural science. But psychology was not very scientific. The economists thought it provided too unsteady a foundation for economics, who make assumption to utility led to a movement to the psychology from economics. In the early part of the 20th century, economists still included rich speculations about
how people feel and think about economic choices generally. However, later economists are very much appealed to psychological insights, but by the middle of the century discussions of psychology had largely disappeared. Throughout the second half of the century, many criticisms of the positivistic perspective took place in both economics and psychology. The economists of the time had less disagreement with psychology with psychology than they realized. They assume without foundation that behavior always aims at the goal of maximum pleasure and minimum pain; but behavior is not goal-oriented. Also the economists of the time believed false conclusions are drawn from false psychological assumptions. The importance of psychological measures and bounds on rationality. These commentators attracted attention, but did not alter the fundamental direction of economics. One development was the rapid acceptance by economists of the expected utility and discounted utility models which are making decision under uncertainty and choice, respectively. Whereas the assumptions and implications of utility analysis are rather flexible, and the expected utility and discounted utility models have numerous precise and testable implications. As a result, they provided some of the first "hand targets" for critics of the standard theory.

As economists began to accept counterexamples that could be not be permanently ignored, developments in psychology identified promising directions for new theory. Beginning around 1960 year, psychology became dominated by the brain as an information-processing device replacing the behaviorist conception of the brain as a stimulus-response machine. The information-processing permitted a fresh study of neglected topics like memory, problem solving and decision making. These new topics were more obviously relevant to the conception of utility maximization than behaviorism had appeared to be. However, psychologists began to use economic models as a benchmark against which their psychological models. Early research in behavioral have followed. First, identify assumption or models that are used by economists, who expected utility and discounted utility. Second, the assumption or model is a rule out alternative explanations (such as subjects' confusion or transactions costs). And third, the assumption or model creates alternative theories that generalize existing models. The fourth step is to construct economic models of behavior using the behavioral assumptions to test them from the third step. This final step of economic models of behavior has only been taken more recently to apply.

Experimental control method measures consumption behavior

The methods in behavioral economics are the same as those in other areas of economies. In fact, behavioral economics relied heavily on evidence generated by experiments. More recently, however, behavioral economists have moved beyond experimentation and the full range of methods are employed by economists. The experiments played a large role in the initial phase of behavioral economics because experimental control is exceptionally helpful for distinguishing behavioral explanations from standard ones. Suppose we observed this phenomenon in these any one of cares, in the form of failures of legal cases to settle before trial, costly divorce proceedings, and labor strikes. They are phenomenon of human' behaviors are caused by costs and benefits measurement of result. Also, behavioral economy would be difficult to tell whether rejection of offers was the result of reputation-building in repeated games, agency problems (between clients and lawyers), confusion, or an expression of distaste for being treated unfairly. However, in these game experiments of failures of legal cases to settle before trial, costly divorce proceedings, and labor strikes. The first three of these explanations are ruled out because the experiments are played once, have no agents, and are simple enough to rule out confusion. Thus, the experimental data clearly establish that subjects are expressing concern for fairness. Other experiments have been useful for testing whether judgment errors which individuals commonly make in psychology experiments also affect prices and quantities in markets. The lab is especially useful for these studies because individual and market-level data can be observed. Although behavioral economists relied on experimental data, however, behavioral economics subject is seen as a very different method from experimental economics. As noted, behavioral economists are methodological profession. They define themselves, not on the basis of the research methods that who employ, but rather their application of psychological insights to economics. Experimental economists, on the other hand, define themselves on the basis of use of experimentation which is as a research tool. Also, economists have made a major investment in developing experimental methods that are suitable for addressing economic issues, and have achieving among themselves on a number of important issues. For example, experimental economists often make instructions and software available for precise replication, and raw data are typically shared for reanalysis. Experimental economists also insist on paying performance-based. However, experimental economists have also developed rules that many behavioral economists are likely to find excessively . For example, experimental economists rarely collect data like demographics, self-reports, response times and other cognitive measure which behavioral economists have found useful. Descriptions of the experimental environment are usually abstract rather than which are carried on experiment in the outside world because economic theory rarely makes a prediction about how a happen would matter, and experimenters are concerned about losing control over incentives if choosing strategies with certain labels is appealing.

Finally, economic experiments also typically use "stationary replication", in which the same task is repeated over and over in each period. Data from the last few periods of the experiment are typically used to draw conclusions about equilibrium behavior outside the lab. When economists believe that examining behavior after it is of great interest, it is also obvious that many important aspects of economic life are like the first few periods of an experiment rather than the last. Supposing if we need to make decision of marriage, educational decisions, and saving for retirement, or the purchase of large durables like houses, sailboats, can cars, which happen just a few times in a person's life, a focus on behavior is clearly not warranted. All said, the focus on psychological realism and economic applicability of research promoted by the behavioral-economics perspective suggests the usefulness research outside the lab and of a broader range of approaches to laboratory research. So, economists realize that who have ideal opportunity to learn by trial-and-error, in a stationary environment, and uses the opportunity to learn how to carry on experimenting any psychology and behavioral researches.

Judgement and choice influences behavioral consumption

The field of behavioral decision research, on which behavioral economics has drawn more than any other subfield of psychology, typically classifies research into two categories: judgement and choice. Judgement research deals with the processes people use to estimate probabilities. Choice deals with the processes people use to select among actions, considering of any relevant judgements who may have made. Everyday, we need to make probable judgements. Due to judging the likelihood of events is central to economic life. For example: Will you lose your job in a poor economic environment? Will you be able to find another house you like as much as the one you must bid for right away? Will the government raise interest rates? Will a merger strategy increase profits? These questions are answered by some process of judging likelihood. The standard principles used in economic to model probability judgement in economic are concepts of statistical sampling, which are concerned probabilities in the face of new evidence. However, it requires a separation between previously judged probabilities and evaluations of new evidence. However, people often overestimate the probability who previously attached to events which later happened. This leads to "second guessing". For example, Monday morning quarterbacking and may be partly responsible for lawsuits against stockbrokers who lost money for their clients. (The clients think the brokers should have known). For example, anybody has tried to learn from a computer manual has seen the curse of knowledge in action. Another example for making probability judgements is called "representativeness": People judge conditional probabilities like P(hypothesis /data) or P(example/class) by how well the data represents the hypothesis or the example represents the class. Representativeness is an economical shortcut that delivers reasonable judgements with minimal effort in many cases. For example, in judging whether a certain student described in a profile is, say, a psychology major or computer science major, the student decides how well the profile matches the psychology or computer science .

Many studies show how this sort of feature-matching can lead people to under weigh the "base rate", in this example, the overall frequency of the two majors. Another by product of representativeness is the "law of small numbers": Small samples are though to represent the properties of the statistical process that generated them (as if the law of large numbers, which guarantees that a large sample of independent draws does represent the process, is in a hurry to work). If a baseball player get hits 30% of his times at bat, but is 0 for 4 , so far in a particular game, then he is "due" for a hit in his next at bat in this game, so that this game's hitting profile will more closely represent his overall ability. Field and experimental studies with basketball shooting and betting on games that people believe that there is positive attitude that players experience the "hot hand", when there is no evidence that such an effect exists. For example, judgements of the fairness or non misleading or reasonable of clients‘ financial report to accounting auditors, consumers buying products and classroom negotiation. It is important to judge whether it is both a good attitude and bad attitude. A good attitude provides fast, close to optimal, answers when time or capabilities are limited, but it also needs logical principles and leads to situations. So, optimal is largely a critique (a reasonable one) of the later applied research. Assume that people specify a set of hypotheses, or encode new evidence incorrectly. For example, assuming that people believe hypothesis A is more likely than B will never encode pro-A evidence mistakenly, but will sometimes encode pro-B evidence as being supportive. For another example, investors will think there is wide variation in skill of, say, mutual-fund managers, even if there is no variation at all. (A manager who does well several years is a surprise if performance is mistakenly thought due to non replacement, so concluding that the manager must be really good.) A question concerns stock market, such as: Overreacts in the long term. In their model, earnings follow a random walk but investors believe, mistakenly, that earnings have positive attitude. After one or two periods of good earnings, the stock market can not be confident that exists and hence expects, but since earnings are really a random walk, the stock market is too pessimistic and is underreacting to good earnings news. After a good earnings, however, the stock market believes many investors are increasing. Since, it is not the stock market is too optimistic and overreact. For another example, valuable consumer products (A $100 wireless keyboard, a fancy computer mouse, bottles of wine, and a box of chocolate) are sold to postgraduate (MBA) business students. The students were presented with a product and asked whether who would buy it for a price equal to the last two digits of their own social security number (a roughly random identification number required to obtain work in the United States) converted into a dollar figure, e.g. , if the last digits were 99, then the postgraduate business students will accept the hypothetical price was $99 to buy any of it for a price to the last two digits of their own social security number . After giving a yes/no response to the question. Would you pay $99? subjects were asked to state the most who would pay (using a procedure that gives people an incentive to say what who really would pay). Although subjects were reminded that the social security number is essentially random, those with high numbers were willing to pay more for the products. However, many studies have also shown that the method used to elicit preferences can have dramatic consequences. Nevertheless, when required to make an economic decisions-to-choose a brand of toothpaste, a car, a job, or how to invest, people do make some kind of decision. Behavioral economists refer to the process by which people make choices with ill defined preferences as "constructing preferences".

However, in classical consumer theory, preferences among different commodities are assumed to be invariant with respect to an individual's current consumption. Specifically, people seem to dislike losing commodities from their consumption much more than they like gaining other commodities. For example, the research of "contingent valuation" studies that attempt to establish the dollar value of products which are not routinely trades. Contingent valuation is often used to do government cost-benefit analysis or establish legal penalties from environment damage. These surveys typically show very large differences between buying prices (e.g. paying to clean up oil of beaches) and selling prices (e.g. having to be paid to allow beaches to be ruined).

Nowadays, a quarter of the wealth in the USA has more interesting opportunities to do behavioral economies. They find that motivated sellers should regard the price who paid as a sunk cost and choose at a nominal loss from the purchase price. Sellers' listing prices and subsequent selling behavior reflects to nominal losses. There are some cases in which no effect would be expected, such as when products are purchased for resale rather than for utilization. For example, Do art or antique dealers like with pieces who buy to resell? What about surrogate mothers who agree to bear a child for a price paid in advance? However, evidence on the degree of commercial attachment is mixed. Reference points can also serve as social focal points for judging performance. For an interesting example from corporate finance. In general, when managers whose firms face possible losses (or declines from a previous year's earnings) are very reluctant to report small losses. As a result, the distribution of actual losses and gains show a very large at zero, and hardly any small reported losses (compared to the number of small gains). A manager who does not have the skill to shift accounting profits to erase a potential loss (i.e. has some earnings in his pocket.) is considered a poor manager. It seems that the bad performance manager whose behavior is bad to mislead public to believe his firm have better performance in this year. Hence, in the mental accounting view, people set up mental accounts for outcomes which are psychologically separate, much as financial accountants lump expenses and revenues into separated accounts to guide managerial attention. Otherwise, mental accounting stands in opposition to the standard view in economics that it predicts, accurately , that people will spend money coming from different sources in different ways. So, a generalization of the notion of mental accounting is the concept of "choice bracket" , which refers to the fashion in which people make decisions narrowly, in either a piece meal fashion, or board, i.e. taking account of interdependencies between decisions. For example, when making many separate choices between products, consumers tend to choose more diversity when the choices are bracketed broadly than when they are bracketed narrowly.

Expected utility theory estimates behavioral consumption

The expected utility (EU) hypothesis explains that the utility of a risky distribution of outcomes (says, monetary payoffs) is a probability weighted average of the outcome utilities. It follows logically from apparently reasons. Most notably the independence (or " cancellation") choice. The independent choice says that if you are comparing two gambles, you should cancel events which lead to the same consequence with the same probability, your choice should be independent of those utility also simplifies matters because a person's taste for risky money distributions can be fully captured by the share of the utility function for money.

However, many studies document predictive failures of expected utility in simple situations in which subjects can earn substantial sums of money from their choices. Some of these new theories alter the way in which probabilities are weighted, but preserve a "between ness" property which says that if A is preferred to B, then any probabilistic gamble between them must be preferred to B, but dis preferred to A (i.e. the gambles like "between" A and B in preference). Other new theories suggest that probability weights are "rank-dependent", outcomes are first ranked, then their probabilities are weighted in a way which is sensitive to how who rank within the gamble that is being considered. For example, if a person is attitude towards gambles really came from the utility of wealth function, even large gains in wealth would not tempt who to risk $50 or $100 losses, if who really dislikes losing $10 more than who likes gaining $11 at every level of wealth. For example, linear probability weighting in expected utility (EU) works reasonably well except when outcome probabilities are very low or high. But low-probability events are important in the economy in the form of "gambles" with positive (lottery tickets and also risky business ventures in biotechnology and pharmaceuticals) and high risk compensation events which required large insurance industries. Another theory example, such as prospect theory is experimental choices more accurately than (EU) because it gets the psychological of judgement and choice right. It consists of two main components, a probability weighting function, and a "value function" which replaces the utility function of (EU). The weighting function P(P) combines two elements: (1) The level of probability weight is a way of expressing risk tastes (if you hate to gamble, you will place low weight on any chance of winning anything) and (2) P(P) captures how sensitive people are to differences in probabilities. If people are move sensitive in the neigh hoods of possibility and certainty. i.e. changes in probability near zero and 1, then their P(P) curve will overweight low probabilities and underweight high ones. For another theory example, such as technical motivation for "rank dependent" theories, ranking outcomes, than weighting their probabilities is that when separate probabilities are weighted, it is easy to construct examples in which people will be dominance by choosing a "dominated" gamble A which has a lower chance of winning at each possible outcome amount, compared to the higher chance of winning the same outcome amount for a dominant gamble B. If people rarely choose such dominated gambles, who are acting as if who are weighting the differences in probabilities which is the essence of the rank dependent approaches. So, new information can help any decision maker to feel better to make better decisions. These theories effect may explain demand for information in settings like medicine or personal finance, where new information usually does not change choice, but relieves anxiety people have from knowing there is something who could know but don't. However, the planning problem for economic agents who would like to behave in fashion and discussed the important time discounting for choice. Most big decisions, e.g. savings, educational investments, labor supply, health and diet, crime and drug etc. decisions use have costs and benefits which occur at different point in time. Thus, time discounting is basically standard time discounting plus an immediacy effect, a decision discounts delays in equally at all moments except the current one, caring differently about well being. This functional form provides one sample and powerful model of the taste to individual to make right or reasonable behavior economic decision. However, most analyses of choice assume that people integrate new consumption with planned consumption. It is infeasible and perhaps for this reason, descriptively inaccurate. When people make decisions about new sequences of payments or consumption, they tend to evaluate them in isolation, e.g. treating negative outcomes as losses, rather than as reductions to their existing money flows or consumption plans.

How to decide fairness and social preferences. The assumption that people maximize their own wealth and other personal material goals just self-interest is a correct simplification that is often useful in economics. However, people may sometimes choose to spend their wealth to punish others who have harmed them, reward whose, so who have helped, or to make outcomes more fair. Just as understanding demand for products requires specific utility function, the key to understanding this sort of social preferences is a specification of social utility which can explain many types of date with a single function.

Behavioral economy can also use to assist firms to choose right behavior to decide to do any matters. I show hypothesis to establish any reference level of consumer surplus and product profit. Both sides are entitled to any firm's levels of profit, so price changes which threaten any matter are considered unfair. So raising any product price, it will reduce consumer surplus and is considered unfair. But the cost of a firm's inputs rises, subjects said it was fair to raise prices. Because not raising prices would reduce the firm's profit (compared to the reference profit). Everyday observation that firms don't change prices and wages as frequently commonly. For example, when the fourth Hary potter story book was released in summer 2000 year, most stores were allocated a small number of books that were pre-sold in advance. Why not raise prices or auction the books off? It is possible that it concerned about customer goodwill and excess demand to cause book stores limit such book price increases. Offended consumers are often able to affect firm behavior by media attention or provoking legislation. For example, scalping tickets for popular sports and entertainment events (resulting them at a large premium over the printed ticket price) is constrained by law in most countries. For example, some countries have "anti-laws" penalizing sellers who take advantage of shortages of water, fuel and other necessities by raising prices after natural disasters. So, the countries' governments can protect which citizen benefits to balance the natural resource supply and demand to sell in the reasonable price fairly after the natural disaster occurrence.

A few years ago, responding to public anger at rising CEO salaries when the economy was being restructured through downsizing and many workers lost their jobs. Otherwise, some countries passed a law prohibiting firms from deducting CEO salaries for tax purposes beyond $1 million a year. because the countries need to earn much tax income from these high salary CEO income every year. So, explaining why these laws and regulations come from is one example of now economics might be used to expand the scope of law and behavioral economic relationship.

How behavioral game theory influences shareholder's individual investment behavior

Game theory has rapidly become an important foundation for many areas of economic theory, such as bargaining in decentralized markets, contracting and organizational structure. The descriptive accuracy of game theory in these application can be questioned because equilibrium predictions often assume strategic reasoning and direct field tests are difficult. In fact, behavioral game theory uses any experimental evidence and psychological research to generalize the standard assumptions of game theory. One component of behavioral game theory is a theory of social preferences for allocations of money to oneself and others. Another component is a theory of how people choose in one shot games or in the first period of a repeated game. For example, in share buying and selling market, shareholders shall buy or sell shares from their judgement in the economic cycle market everyday. So share investment is seemed as allocation of game to these shareholders. Also, shareholders whose mind can influence whose psychological behavior to decide how to invest whose shares in their share investment economic activities. The component of behavioral game theory can include a model of learning to either individual or a population. Also, game theory is one area of economy in which serious attention has been paid to the process by which can equilibrium comes about. Many learning theories have been proposed and carefully tested with experimental data. Theories about population never predict as well as theories of individual learning through who are useful for other purposes. So, behavioral game theory can be applied to these complex environments. e.g. consumer supermarket purchase, share market etc. How to apply behavioral game theory to macroeconomics and saving aspect? Many concepts in macroeconomic probably have a behavioral style that could be influenced by research in psychology. For example, it is common to assume that prices and wages are in nominal terms, which has important implications for macroeconomic behavior. Behavioral economics suggests some ideas for among consumers and workers, perhaps it is influenced by workers' concern for fairness. An important model in macroeconomics is the life cycle model of savings or permanent income hypothesis. This theory assumes that people make a guess about their lifetime earnings profile, and plan their lifetime earnings profile, and plan their savings and consumption in each period has diminishing marginal utility; and preferences for consumptions streams are time-separable (i.e. overall utility is the sum of the discounted utility of consumption in each separate period). The theory also assumes people lump together different types income when they guess how much money who will have (i.e. different sources of wealth are different). So, why many young people won't spend too much money for unnecessary expenditure, e.g. entertainment easily. Because who plan to save for their old age to use in their long time life time.

A behavioral life cycle theory of savings in which different sources of income are kept track of in different mental accounts. Mental accounts can reflect natural perceptual or divisions. For example, it is possible to add up the travelers' pay check and dollar value of whose frequent flyer miles, but it is simply unnatural to do so. It is important to note that many key implications of the life-cycle hypothesis have never been well supported (e.g. consumption is far more closely related to current income than it should be according to theory. However, predictions can be improved by introducing utility functions with habit formation in which utility in a current depends on the reference point of previous consumption, and by more carefully accounting for uncertain about future income. So, mental accounting is only one of several behavioral approaches that may prove useful. Economics is money illusion, it is the tendency to make decisions based on nominal quantities rather than converting those figures into real terms by adjusting for inflation. Money illusion seems to be pervasive in some domains. So, it appears that employees don't seem to mind if their real wage falls as long as their nominal wages doesn't fall. Labor macroeconomics is involuntary unemployment. Why can some people not find work beyond of switching jobs, or a natural rate of unemployment? A popular account of unemployment push that wages are deliberately paid above the market clearly level, which creates an excess supply of workers and hence unemployment. But why are wages too high ? As efficiency wage theory shows that paying workers more than who deserve is necessary to ensure that who have something to lose if they are unemployed, which motivates them to work hand and economizes on monitoring. Another viewpoint indicates that employer and worker is such as into a gift exchange relationship. Employers pay more than who have to as a gift and workers repay the gift by working harder than necessary. They show how gift exchange can be an equilibrium and show some of its macroeconomic implications. In labor economics, gift exchange is clearly evident of experimental labor markets. In practical working environment, firms offer wages; workers who take the jobs than choose a level of effort, which is costly to the workers and valuable to the firms. For example, firms and workers can enforce wages, but not effort levels. Since workers and firms are matched for just one period, and do not learn each other's identities, there is no way for either side to build reputations or for firms to punish workers who chose low effort. However, self interested workers should shirk, and firms should anticipate that and pay a low wage. In fact, firms deliberately pay high wages as gifts and workers choose higher effort levels when they take higher wage jobs. It seems that it has strong relationship between wages and effort is stable over time. For example, standard life-cycle theory assumes that if people can borrow they should prefer wage profiles which maximize the present value of lifetime wages. Holding total wage payments constant, and assuming a positive real rate of interest, present value maximization implies that workers should prefer declining wage profiles over increasing ones. However, in fact, most wages profiles are clearly rising over time which is such as a phenomenon. Rather, workers derive utility from positive changes in consumption, but have self-control problems. That would prevent them from positive changes in consumption, but have self-control problems that would prevent them from saving for later consumption of wages were more front-loaded in the life cycle. In addition, workers seem to derive positive utility from increasing wage profiles, it is perhaps because rising wages are a source of self-esteem and the desire for increasing payments is much weaker for non wage income. The standard life-cycle of labor supply also implies that workers should substitute labor and leisure based on the wage rate who face and the value who place on leisure at different points in time. If wage fluctuations are temporary workers should work long hours when wages are high and short hours when wages are low. However, because changes in wages are often persisting and because work hours are generally fixed in the short-run. So, it is difficult to tell whether workers are substituting. For example, taxi drivers who target daily will drive longer hours on low income days and guilty early on high income days. This behavior is exactly the opposite of substitution. Also inexperienced taxi drivers support the daily targeting prediction. But experienced taxi drivers don't have negative elastic, either because target minded drivers earn less and self select or taxi drivers learn over time to substitute rather than target. Perhaps the simplest prediction of labor economics is that the supply of labor should be upward sloping in response to a increase in wage.

In finance, standard equilibrium models of asset pricing assume that investors only care about asset risks if who affect marginal publicly available information to forecast stock returns as accurately as possible the efficient markets hypothesis. When those hypotheses do make some accurate predictions and some investors in assets have limited rationality of behavioral finance. Also, in share stock market, it is common, shareholders should not want to trade with them, but the volume of stock market transaction is large. So, it presents data on individual trading behavior which suggests that the extremely high volume may be driven, in part, by overconfidence on the part of investors. For example, property agent's individual behavior is similar to share agent's individual behavior. In the economy view, property agent bases a list price for a house on the selling prices of nearly houses that is similar ("comparable"). Every nearest neigh our techniques bases on similarity is also used in credit scoring and other kinds of evaluations. Also, one firm whose every share sale on the selling price is comparable to its similar firms whose every share price in its same business industry. The shareholder will evaluate whose every share issued sale price in the stock (share) market. Otherwise, in behavioral economy view, for example, property or share buyer who has risky choice to decide to buy in the property or share market. It is a process of comparing the similarity of the probabilities and outcomes in two gambles and choosing on dimensions which are dissimilar.

As we mentioned above, behavioral economics simply includes an interest in psychology. In fact, we believe that many familiar economic distinctions do have a lot of behavioral content, they are implicitly behavioral, and could surely benefit from more explicit ties to psychological ideas and data. However, some people do not feel psychology and economy which have close relationship. Such as, substantial debate is ongoing in psychology about whether knowing the precise details of how the brain carries out computations is necessary to understand functions and mechanisms of driving car skill at higher levels, (knowing the mechanical details of how a car works may not be necessary to turn the key and drive it). Most psychology experiments use indirect measures like response times, error self reports and natural experiments, due to brain has been fairly successful in codifying what we know about thinking, but pessimists think brain scan studies won't add much. The optimists think the new tools will lead to some discoveries. Another couple is the distinction between short run and long run price elasticity which concerns behavioral economy. In fact, economy needs have theories concepts to support any evidence to prove any matter has happened. Concerning short run and long run price elasticity cause and effort issue, with a casual suggestion that the run is the time it takes for markets to adjust, or for consumers to learn new prices, after a demand or supply stock. Adjustment costs undoubtedly have technical and social component, but probably also have some behavioral factors influence in the form of gradual adaption to loss and learning.

Another macroeconomic model which can be interpreted as implicitly behavioral is that business cycles can emerge if it is not general price inflation, so why the consumers shall not decide to buy this kind of product in the competitive market. For example, risky choice is as a process of comparing the similarity of the probabilities and outcomes in two gambles, and choosing on dimensions which are dissimilar. Behavioral economic simply includes an interest in psychology. In fact, we believe that many familiar economic distinctions do have a lot of behavioral content, they are implicitly behavioral and could surely benefit from more explicit ties to psychological ideas and data. However, some people do not feel psychology and economy which have close relationship. Such as psychology is about whether knowing the precise details of how the brain carries out computations is necessary to understand functions and mechanisms at higher levels. (knowing the mechanical details of how a car works may not necessary to turn the key and drive it.) Most psychology experiments use indirect measures like response times, error rates, self reports and natural experiments due to brain has been fairly successful in codifying what we know about thinking. However, pessimists think brain scan studies won't add much. The optimists think the new tools will lead to some discoveries and the potential is great that they cannot be ignored. However, economy needs have theories or concepts to support evidence to prove why any matters had happened. An example, is the distinction between short term and long term price elasticity. This distinction, mentions between of them, with a casual suggestion that long run is the time it takes for markets to adjust, or for consumers to learn new prices, after a demand or supply shock. Adjustment costs undoubtedly have technical and social components, but probably also have some behavioral factors influence in the form of gradual adaption to loss and learning.

However, organizational behavioral theory concerns that organizational contracting are shot through with implicitly behavioral economics. Some economists motivate the incompleteness of contracts as a consequence of rationality in foreseeing the future, but do not tie the research directly to work on memory and imagination. For example, agency theory begins with the presumption that there is some activity the agent doesn't like to do. Why markets are better at making dramatic changes than managers influence cost. So, influence costs are the costs managers preform for projects who like or personally benefit from like promotion or raises. A lot of influence costs are undoubtedly inflated by optimistic, each division manager really does think their division desperately needs funds and social comparison of pay and benefits. Otherwise, why are salaries kept so secret? In all these cases, conventional economic behavior has deeper psychological questions of where adjustment costs, effort and influence costs come from. So, it beings these questions: Could these phenomena surely produce surprising testable prediction? Is psychology regularity an assumption or a conclusion?

Behavioral economics generally begins with assumption rooted in psychological regularity and asks what follows from those assumptions. An alternative approach is to work backward, regarding a psychological regularity as a conclusion that must be proved an explanation that must be derived from deeper assumption before we fully understand and accept it. The alternative approach is caused by a fashionable new direction in economic theory and psychology too, which is to explain human behavior as the product of evolution. However, we may not believe that behavior of intelligent, modern people lived in socialization and cultural influence can only be understood by guessing what their lives were like and how their brains might have adapted generally. There are other models that treat psychological regularity as a conclusion to be proved rather than an assumption to be used. Such models usually begin with an observed regularity. Economists have for deriving behavior from first principles and rationalizing apparent irrationality. Theories of this sort are useful behavioral economics and what fresh predictions do they make. However, critics have pointed out that behavioral economics is not a unified theory, but is instead a collection of tools and ideas. This is true. However, some economists believe that economic models do not derive much predictive power from the single tool of utility maximization. The goal of behavioral economic is to develop better tools that, in some cases, can do both jobs at once. Economists like to point out the natural division of labor between scientific disciplines: Psychologists should concern to individual minds, and economists to behavior in games, markets, and economies. But the division of labor is only efficient if there is effective coordination, and all too often economists fail to conduct intellectual trade with those who have a comparative advantage in understanding individual human behavior. The only question is whether the implicit psychology in economics is good psychology or bad psychology. We think it is simply unwise, and inefficient to do economics without paying some attention to good psychology.

How to apply behavioural economic principles to assist policy makers or decision makers

Behavioural economics theories can also apply to assist any policy makers to make right and reasonable decision in right time. I shall indicate new principles to recommend and I also shall give any psychological cases to explain how policy makers can apply behavioural economic theories to judge how to make their any decision is the most right and the most reasonable.

Behavioural economy is an independent and demonstrates real economic well-being. It aims to improve quality of life by promoting innovative solutions that challenge mainstream thinking on economic, environment and social issues. Also, behavioural economy is different branches of more alternative economies into a form that is useful primarily for policy-makers. I think behavioural economy can be given an aid to policy makers how who use economic tools to the broader policy making community by providing a theoretical behaviour for many policy approaches to be used. The standard economic analysis assumes that humans are rational and behave in a way to maximize their individual self-interest. This rational man assumption indicates a powerful tool for analysis. However, it has many shortfalls that can lead to unrealistic economic analysis and policy-making. Also, I think behavioural economics and psychology has these principles to influence human behaviour. These principles include, such as below:

In common, people do many things by observing others and copying; people are encouraged to continue to do things when they feel other people approve of their behaviour. People do many things without consciously thinking about time. These habits are hard to change. There are cases where money is de-motivating as it undermines people's intrinsic motivation. People want their actions and commitments to be values usually. People put undue weight on recent events and who can't calculate probabilities well and worry too much about unlikely events and who are strongly influences by how the problem/information is presented to them. People need to feel effective to make a change, even just giving who the incentives and information is not necessarily enough in any environment usually. So policy makers ought concern about these human behaviour principles to judge whose behaviours are right or wrong, then who can decide to do any economic activities more reasonable, e.g. decisions of consumption, policies making, investment etc.

In fact, much of our behaviour is strongly influenced by other people's behaviour. Social learning is a process by which we take in the behaviour of others to learn how to behave. In more complex situations with which we are unfamiliar, we consciously watch and learn from the behaviour of others. For example, when use a new library for the first time. When we mist make a conscious decision on how to behave, our sense of social identity is important, we think: how would other from my group behave in this situation? In situations where there is high social capital. i.e. where there are strong networks between people and a high level of mutual trust, so its seems other people's behaviour and our sense of social identity may be extremely important in influencing our own behaviour and policy makers ought need to know how to judge their behaviour whether their behaviour is either right and reasonable or wrong and unreasonable in any learning process of environment. The standard economic theory is tried to explain where people's preferences come from, so it does not take account of the direct influence of the people's behaviour and social norms on our behaviour. The theory assumes we independently know what we want and that our preferences are fixed. This standard theory is very good at explaining short-term decision making. For example, I want green vegetables and choose fruits as they are on special offer, but it cannot explain longer term changes in preferences. I now only choose organic food. Along the same lines the importance of institutions, such as regulations, for example, how people organize markets and the evolution of the whole economic system are not subjects of general economic analysis. This has significant implications for policy design.

In fact, the standard economic theory also assumes that people carry out a full rational analysis of all consumers' available options. This is not what we do; we often just copy the actions of other people. For example, it would require too much effort to look up all the rules when driving in a new country, to find out all the fines/punishments for failing to meet the rules, to work out the probability of being caught and the possible costs, before deciding how to drive there. Instead we just copy other people, and perhaps adjust our behaviour according to the feedback we receive. However, some psychologists indicate to see people how to behave, in especial in crises situations and when others are experts. These psychologists have identified that we are open to influence from people in authority or people we like. When we are influenced by authority, an expert, someone with legitimate power to direct our actions, someone who can either reward or punish us. The effects are less likely to be lasting than we are influenced by someone we like.

However, some people's psychological behaviour is similar to economic behaviour to judge to make any decision. For example, why do you wear a seatbelt in your car? Most of us wear seatbelts as it has became normal behaviour, everyone does it. We neither evaluate the likelihood of having an accident, nor the chance of getting caught without our seatbelt on and incurring a fine. The enforcement of seatbelt wearing is now hardly necessary, as it has become a social norm. What does this mean for policy makers? Policy makers focusing only on economic analysis may often devise a system that has an immediate effect. In psychologists view this issue point, knowing that there is a fine for speeding and a high likelihood of getting caught, the driver will probably drive more slowly, but who will drive just as fast one who realize the chance of being caught is low. However, of policy makers can change the social norm, perhaps in this case by encouraging us to frown on others who drive dangerously fast with campaigns against dangerous driving, then less enforcement will be needed after the change. In other words policy makers might want to take preferences as fixed in the short term, but they should consider shifting preferences in the medium term. An example where policy appears to have successfully changes people's preferences in the US and Singapore and Hong Kong is banning smoking in public places. This change appears to reduce the social proof of the amount people smoke in private places and public places both also. It seems that government policies can influence the decreasing numbers of consumers require to buy cigarette to smoke habitually, due to fine and punishment is regulated to be ban effectively. Such daily routines quickly became habits. Even when we consciously think about what we do, it can be difficult to change our behaviour. Perhaps I think it is a good idea for people to use public transport, but I do not know where the bus stop is or when the bus runs. I think to use private car to drive to work place is more preference choice. The reward feeling , my journey by car was easy and free to reinforce my old bad habit. Psychologists theories on changing habits generally involve raising it to a conscious level where we can consider the merits of alternative behaviour. This is followed by adopting the new behaviour, which, with time, becomes frozen as a new habit. Thus, I think that we need have regulation to control my behaviour, then we can change my behaviour to be new habit from old habit of behaviour easily. For example, human blood sale is an economic product, due to paying donors for blood would increase supply. Supplies would be provided at a cost advantage in the future, if demand continued to rise. Such as supplies to hospitals for blood will has cost from donors when there are many patients need much blood to use to treat any diseases in any hospitals. Otherwise, if there are not many patients need much blood to use, but there are many donors have effort to provide blood to any hospitals, then it will be economic inefficiency and it is highly wasteful of blood. Thus, the blood donors whose blood supplies of behaviour and the cost of blood which will concern to the hospitals patients‘ numbers of demand, so their behaviour and economy has close relationship in the hospital blood demand market.

For shareholder behaviour example, if you hold some shares in a firm that has gone down in value. What do you do?

Many people hold on to their shares in this situation, in the hope that they will recoup their losses. Conversely, when shares have gone up in share, people are happy to sell them to realize their gain, A similar behaviour is also observed for professional traders who tend to hold on to shares with a loss for longer than those with a gain. The traders who exhibit this type of loss to a lesser degree tend to be the more successful ones. For another example, this is a case where the theory is directly applicable within economic cost-benefit-type analyses that include valuations of no-market products, such as valuations of pollution damage. Policy makers have a choice as to whether-to-accept, and as these may vary by up to a factor, the outcome of such an analysis many well depend on which value is chosen. When a policy maker reasonably has a right to something that might be taken away from them, the willing-to-accept value would be used. On the other hand, when the policy maker only reasonable has a right to the status quo and an improvement is proposed, then the willingness-to-pay is the correct value to use.

What behavioral economic preferences regarding time discounting theory would pay and the conclude that the discounted psychologists have long established utility model, which continues to be that people don't make decisions in widely used by economists, has little the way assumed. In generally, people are expected to rationally make the best choices given their preferences, independent of how these choices are presented. Therefor more information and choice is always considered good. Using this theory, policy makers should ensure that people always have as much information and as many things to choose between as possible, the process of introducing policy is irrelevant. Ideas from behavioral economic indicate, however that this is not the right approach.

However, we know from experimental economics that more choice and more information can lead to a feeling of helplessness or reduced self-efficiency. Hence, if people hope have better solutions to a problem. Instead, providing people with opportunities for understanding, exploration and participation engages powerful motivations for competence, being needed. In summary, people 's self-efficacy increases and they are motivated toward implementing the solutions. i.e. changing their behaviour in a desired way. So, a participatory approach not only improves policy, it also makes to any policy makers more happier. In most cases these principles cannot be used directly as part of any mathematical economics analysis, but highlight situations where this standard analysis will not accurately describe human behaviour and therefore might have unintended consequences when implemented in policy. However, that the policy implications could be quite powerful as the behavioural approach provides quite different lines of analysis to the standard economic model. It is heartening to see policy makers focusing more on the psychology of behaviour when devising policy. So behavioural economics is a relatively new field of economics that attempts to incorporate insights from psychology into economic models and analyses. As above cases seem any policy maker's economic activities which are relative to whose psychology's decision. However, psychologists are often interest in understanding at the level of individual or social group of behaviour, the primary interest in economic is usually in understanding how behaviour and interactions play out in a system to shape economic outcomes. Economists are interested in system-level outcomes, such as the level and path of wages, the effect of taxes on economic output, how rates of savings respond to interest rates etc. However, those economic outcomes depend on complex interactions of individuals. So, behavioural economy concerns to how to judge individual to do the reasonable or right behaviour to hope to get the reasonable economic result as well as it's goal rather to help improve any policy makers to understand their behaviour in ways that allow economists to make better predictions and suggest better economic policies. However, new elements about information processing or individual preferences might impact economic models and analyses.

Is psychology influencing all field of economics? It is possible that behavioural economy needs theoretical contributions and laboratory evidence to support to make any reasonable or right decision to any policy makers. This type of work generally uses existing observational data and estimates relationships between variables of interest by either using naturally occurring variation in the data i.e. natural experiment. Perhaps more than any other field, behavioural economics has had a large impact on finance to the point that behaviour finance is often considered a separate field as opposed to being of behavioural economics. Also, public economic is the study of how government policies influence economic markets. A primary emphasis of public economic involves the topic of taxation. Otherwise, the biggest impact that the behavioural approach has had in economic is the analysis of retirement saving to influence any employees' decisions about their retirement savings. However, when employees can do make any active savings choices to prepare their retirement. If employers can assist whose employees to design any methods to allocate fund, then accumulates interest and is tax free until the retirement funds are withdrawn to every retirement employee. The tax advantage make effort to save for retirement.

Behavioural economic is in understanding how individuals do or do not smooth consumption over time. Smoothing consumption is a standard economic models. It suggests that individuals should borrow or save in order to consume a similar amount throughout one's lifetime. For example, a teacher who is paid a salary 12 months a year, who should not spend all whose salary within one year. Rather, the teacher should smooth whose consumption over the 12 month period. How to allocate to spend pay checks, food and social security payments which concerns the teacher decide to spend whose salary efficiently. Hence, who needs to plan how he shall spend whose one year salary to be reasonable use in the future. Public economic is to understand how people respond to taxation and social benefit programs. This has been an area that has seen an explosion of behavioural work in recent year. i.e. how taxpayers can experience over-withholding and receive tax refunds from tax department.

Policymakers and insurers are also increasingly turning to psychology for approaches to improve health behaviour. Traditionally health-policy focused largely on information provision, assuming that as long as individuals were well informed, their decisions would maximize their health choices. Influential work on the effects of smoking taxes, however, well being of smokers appears to increase with higher taxes to influence health behaviours are not completely rational.

Behavioural economic has also had a small impact on the study of criminal behaviour. For example, individuals are not less likely to commit a crime when who are 18 age and of doing so increases dramatically. However, some economists explain the motivations people have for giving to charity and who understand the psychological motivations for charitable giving. So, it seems that charity award giving has probable to reduce 18 age people who choose to do crime behaviour easily because who feel who have effort to assist charity in their life time.

Industrial organization economists study why firms exist and how which function and compete with each other. Insights and psychology and behavioural economics have made a significant contribution to develop that model the interactions of profit maximizing firms with their customers. In fact, firms often need to evaluate whether their products if prices are needed to set what of price of level is the most reasonable and attractive to customers to choose to buy their products. For example, individuals choose cell phone plans with fixed minute allotments and steep charges for going over the minute limits, but frequently exceed their plan limits. This behaviour is the best explained by a model in which people overestimate the precision of their demand forecasts. So, cell phone firms need to research how cell phone plans with fixed minute allotments and steep charges of cell phone call fee charge plan is the most acceptance method to cell phone clients generally. However, cell phone call charge plan and various cell phone product features and the way cell phone clients allocate their limited attention affects cell phone products markets which are external important factors can influence any cell phone clients why who will choose to use the cell phone call plan because any cell phone will be very large durable product to any cell phone consumer after who choose to buy the cell phone product. Hence, who will not often choose to use the old cell phone firm call charge plan if who feel it provides the excellent cell phone call service and reasonable phone call plan to use to compare other cell phone call plans in the cell phone call market. Hence, the cell phone call firm needs to research why consumers need to choose to use which cell phone call plan among of other cell phone call plans in the cell phone call market. Also, researching the cell phone buyers‘ choice behaviour why who choose to buy the cell phone to use issue, which will have influence to the cell phone buyer why who choose to use the cell phone call charge plan because expensive cell phone is needed to use excellent quality of cell phone call service usually. Otherwise, cheap cell phone is needed to use poor quality of cell phone call service usually. So, cell phone call plan is needed to follow the cell phone quality and price to be used and they ought have direct relationship to influence why the cell phone buyer who chooses to use the cell phone call plan.

Finally, behavioural economic can also apply to be used to labour supply as a motivating in negative or positive labour supply elasticities example. For example, it is possible that taxi drivers work fewer hours when wages are high-consistent with a model of daily income targeting. This finding is that when wages are high (perhaps it is raining and thus it is easy to find people who want a taxi ride), taxi drivers are able to hit their daily target quickly and then go home. However, when wages are low, taxi drivers are not able to hit their target quickly and thus work additional hours in order to hit their target. It means taxi driver's behaviour produce the effect that taxi driver works more when wages are low than when wagers are high. This work has resulted to analyse taxi driver of labour supply decisions with daily reference points in non taxi domains. So, instead of the weather and client numbers and taxi charge factors, the factors of taxi drivers' hours worked and the quality of service is produced is another important factor to influence any taxi drivers' numbers to supply to the taxi market.

Behavioural economic has also influenced the understanding of how staffs can impact worker productivity and job satisfaction. For example, it is possible that poor cooperation can cause worker productivity decreases and it can also cause poor job satisfaction to the worker. So, when working environment can impact productivity, social comparisons can have an impact on job satisfaction as well as the worker's job satisfaction and search intentions are affected by knowing about the salaries of their peers in whose firm. Hence, the worker's positive or negative psychological feeling to whose employers which will have effort to influence whose working performance and productivity to whose firm in possible.

Behavioural economic is increasingly being used in the field of development economics or low income countries. Such as, how Philippines can offer commitment to individuals who wanted to save money in whose country or how Philippines can change to smoking behaviour when commitment devices were offered to Philippine smokers. So, Philippines policy makers need to concern resource scarcity and resource allocation issue to solve how to let its low income level householders can raise to the middle income level to achieve the high income level householders and the low income level householders whose income level is not distant very much.

Whether behavioural economy and psychology which has close relationship.

Finally, I shall analyze whether the relationship between the discipline of behavioural economy and psychology which two branches are totally opposite or if the behavioural theories only extend and complement that mainstream economics. I think study of economics is the behaviour of the complex human beings; this science examines how people choose to act and allocate resources in different market situations. So the economic analysis, is based on the implications that arise from a series of simple assumptions (which are sometimes cited as unrealistic) regarding the human nature. However, in psychological view, the individual is characterized by unlimited rationality and by the ability to follow time consistent, in every situation, his self-interest. In these conditions, behavioural economic attempts to consider a field of analysis in the study of economic phenomena. Because economics deals with the study of human behaviour on the market, it highlights the human character of the science and the fact that, besides of all the patterns and models, the analysis refers to the real individual. It is also behavioural because it attempts to combine approaches from several sciences mainly from economics and psychology, and also from sociology, philosophy, anthropology or biology. This is not an easy mission, in the conditions in which these various disciplines have adopted in time different approaches that became, in many ways, contradictory. So, behavioural economics is that a multidisciplinary approach will increase the explanatory power of economics.

On one hand, there are specialists two argue that behavioural economic is a field of economics that continues the hand, there are others who see it as a distinctive school of thought, which proposes a new paradigm. However, behavioural economists propose a multidisciplinary study, criticize certain assumptions on which the traditional model is built (such as rationality and self-interest, in their unlimited form), resource to experiments (the classical method of psychology) to validate some assumptions, propose new theories (such as the prospect theory) and advance different interpretations of the economic behaviour, e.g. how to maximize consumers satisfy their needs. This issue is concerned to concern consumption of psychology and social economic situation research aspect. Also, I think that behavioural economics can help the economic science by describing more realistically the utility functions of the individuals. This field of study is based rather it is a natural extension of the basic approach. However, it is can be claimed that behavioural economics is also built on the premise that psychology methods and assumptions are equally important. Also, models of behavioural economics, allow the utility to depend on the differences between one's own level and a reference level. People are sensitive to changes and preferences are not stable in time. The vision of behavioural economics concerning the inter-temporal choice (which assumes that individuals prefer immediate gains and delay unpleasant activities) seems to be more appropriate to the human behaviour that the one of the traditional model (which assumes that utility is updated over time).

In conclusion, I shall indicate two theories to explain why economy and psychology has close relationship to influence human do any behavioural economic activities daily. For example, through the prospect theory, behavioural economics adds new parameters to improve the mathematical modelling method, which was advanced by economists for decisions taken under uncertainty. However, the theory also proposes a slightly different interpretation. The results are interpreted by the individual as positive or negative deviations from a reference point, which has a neutral psychological value. Last but not least, in addressing social preferences, behavioural economics adds parameters that increase the concern of decision-makers to also assess their utility function in relation to others. For another example, the choice theory; secondly there is not a common consensus between the specialists of behavioural economics regarding the variables that should be included; and finally, many variables that affect the behaviour are not quantitative, but qualitative, and cannot be precisely measured. The findings of behavioural economic are relevant and can help the mainstream theory by providing a more realistically base of study. However, this argument has contributed to the development of behavioural economics, because there are a large number of phenomena that cannot be entirely explained by the mainstream economics. So, why in the beginning, I indicated why behavioural economics does not imply the totally exclusion of the neoclassical approach and the most studies in this area try to provide a more realistic base of the standard theory. In the concluding, I believe that in time, behavioural economic models will replace the simplified ones, based on unlimited rationality. Also, economists have provided a great importance to the quantitative structures, departing from the human nature. However, behavioural economics can become truly revolutionary only it will always be receptive and will provide a critical insight to their own theories and perspectives, and especially the ones regarding the aspects that they reproach to the traditional economic theory. However, I also feel that the individual's behaviour on the market is determined only be economic factors. In brief, individual choices and, by this, the demand variation are explained only and the variations in the prices of products/ services and the available personal income. Am important discussion in the field of determine directly the economic behaviour of an individual (like the sociological and psychological of factors) are actually active elements in the process the reshaping of the utility functions. Finally, in my view, I believe that the conduct of the market phenomena, as it occurs in reality. In this sense, the research of behavioural economics aims to see how the neoclassical model could be improved, using mainly psychology concepts. Although, there are some specialists who argue that behavioural economics can be an alternative to the neoclassical theory.

Most findings, of my study conducted in this book, modify some of standard economical assumptions, in order to provide a greater psychological realism. However, the additions proposed by behavioural economists simply recognize the human limitations on (mentally) calculations, will and self-interest. So, I think psychology and economy has close relationship to influence any policy makers or decision makers to do any economic psychology daily. Because the purpose of economics is to better understand and explain the conduct of the economic activities as which occur in reality. Otherwise, human being is complex and its behaviour and constitution is studied by all the social sciences. Consequently, multi and interdisciplinary approaches can bring real benefits to the economic science, by providing a more realist foundation to cause any policy makers or decision makers how to decide to make any behaviours or economic activities by behavioural economic activities support daily.

How labour behavior influences economy development

Economics of risky health behaviours can include these personal behaviour, such as smoking, drinking alcohol, drug use, unprotected sex and poor diets is a major source of preventable death. How traditional economics approaches emphasize utility maximization, under certain assumptions which is result of a limited role for policy interventions. Also, non traditional models, e.g. hyperbolic time discounting or bonded rationality how government intervention has greater potential to increase social welfare.

The consequences of risky health behaviours for economic outcomes, such as medical care cost, educational cost, employment wages and crime. Also how policies and strategies modify risky health behaviours, such as taxes or subsidies, cash incentives, restrictions on purchase and use, providing information and restricting advertisement etc. government intervention behaviour. Why health behaviours are important. Because health market includes market products and services, such as medical care, investments of time, environmental conditions, such as air pollution, sanitation and water purity. In special, industrial countries need to concern morality more than infections diseases, health behaviours are particularly important. However, alcohol consumption is also serious in developed countries, e.g. United States, England. Why health behaviour is important. Because tobacco smoking, diet, physical activity and alcohol and drug consumption and useful sexual behaviours, driving and illicit drug use etc. unhealthy behaviour or consumption is increasing to cause many people to be dead easily in developing countries and developed countries both. As a result, many of the risk factors may reflect a combination of health behaviours and medical treatments. For example, high blood pressure has risk factor to be affected by health behaviour, such as smoking, physical in activity and diet. In fact, the risks of death included child underweight, unsafe water sanitation and indoor smoke for solid fuels which are a direct consequence of poverty. However, poverty could affect unhealthy behaviours. So, low income household families play roles of high risk factors to cause who choose to do unhealthy behavior to cause death easily.

Health behaviours, such as physical in activity (no leisure-time physical activity), medical screening tests.

Overall, changes in health behaviours since the 1970 year, particularly the rapid decline in smoking have mostly operated in the direction of improving overall health. However, the race/ethnicity, age, education and annual family income factors can influence health behaviours. Usually, high income and education and Western or Asia race people who are more concerning about their health. So, the countries' governments can spend less expenditure on medical welfare assistance to prepare to them to use when who are old age to reach retirement time. Although, these countries' governments can expand less medical expenditure to give welfare to these kind of people, but their hospitals income will be also decreasing, due to these high income and educational people who are concerning their health to avoid to eat bad foods and eat the health foods, so their sick will be also increasing in their life time, it means that who will not often see doctors, so hospitals' income will also decrease because which will decrease these patient numbers often.

However, differences in health behaviours are one possible explanation for why socio-economic status is positively related to health status and life expectancy. So, it can explain that behaviour is only a small fraction of the better health and longer life expectancy experienced by high individuals with high socio-economic status. It seems behavioural choices increase the estimated effect of behaviours on health outcomes and reduce the death or illness causes. For example, high educated people began to concern to eat health foods, e.g. fruits and vegetables between 1988 year to 1994 year and 1999 year to 2002 year. Hence, it can cause the fresh foods, e.g. vegetables and fruits markets consumption increased, due to the high educational consumers of numbers are increasing because who began to change diet behaviours to choose to buy much fruits or vegetables to eat daily. It is possible that who began to believe those are health foods. Also, some liking driving consumers who liked to drive cars to be relax in their entertainment time. However, due to many doctors promote health message from televisions or radios or newspapers or sport magazines etc. media, such as often walking, running, riding bicycles sports are more health to any people to cause long time life easily. So, these often driving consumers will reduce much time to drive their cars in their leisure or rest time on Sunday or Saturday or holidays. However, who will choose to carry on walking or running or riding bicycles in their leisure or rest time often. So, their physical activities are changed to do sport behaviour from driving their cars of behaviour because who feel sport can be health to them. Otherwise, driving is not health to them. It will cause the oil, gas, electric battery car energy supplied companies income will be decreased because who will not spend much expenditure to buy these energy power to drive their cars often. So, these driving householder families consumer numbers will be decreasing when who choose to spend their rest or relax time to change their driving behaviour to do health physical activities often. It seems consumers who change their behaviours can influence the product or service suppliers' income in possible. So, it seems that consumer health behaviours can caused some businessmen income will be increased, such as vegetables or fruits foods. Otherwise, the beefs foods businessman income will be decreased. When the many consumers change their diet behaviours immediately. For another example, the smoke companies income will be decreased, when many smokers choose to reduce their smoking of numbers every day. Also, the hospitals income will be decreased if many people are health and who have no any diseases, e.g. cancer. So, hospital cancer patients of numbers will reduce. Also, it is possible that hospitals will not employ many cancer doctors because cancer patients of numbers decrease immediately. But in the long term, these countries' governments will avoid to spend much medical welfare allowance to assist many poor householder or low income householder families in the future because it is possible that these are many cancer patients of numbers will decrease. Also, the countries' air pollution will be reduced due to less people have smoke habit. For another example, when many liking driving people who reduce time to drive cars in their relax or rest time when who do not need to drive to work.

So, their cars won't need much oil or gas or electric battery power to consume, it means that these power suppliers will decrease to sell private car oil or gas or electronic battery products to these liking driving householder families. So, it seems consumers' health behaviour can influence the economic income to some businessmen.

The importance of health behaviour in explaining morality in economically developed countries. Smoking, alcohol consumption, drug use consumption behaviours are economic concepts that relate to all behaviours and the important differences across the various health behaviours. The traditional economic approach to studying health behaviours. Basic aspects of the model are that people receive health capital at birth, which depreciates with age, but can be raised through investment, death occurs when the health stock falls below a minimum level. Health has both consumption and investment aspects, as life time is available for market and non market activities. People produce health by combining market products and services with time. For example, on individual might choose to buy sport running shoes and spending time to run on their rest time for relax on Sunday, Saturday or holiday. Individual can allocate time and money to maximize the present discounted value of lifetime utility. Indirectly, length of life is a choice in the original model.

Specially, the timing of death results from conscious decisions regarding health investments made with full knowledge of health education. Assuming that health has only investment aspects, i.e. it doesn't enter the utility function directly and is only valuable for producing healthy days. Health capital is characterized by an equality of the supply of health capital, i.e. the opportunity cost of health capital and the demand for health capital, i.e. the marginal monetary return on health investment. Usually, people invest in such behaviours until the margin, the return on investments in health equals the opportunity cost of health capital.

The model also applies to unhealthy behaviours, as negative investments in health. The marginal costs of the unhealthy behaviour, including both the monetary cost of purchasing market products, such as cigarettes and alcohol and cost of reduced health and shorter life time and the marginal benefits, such as the pleasure derived from consumption of these unhealthy market products, such etc. However, schooling may improve health by enhancing allocative efficiency (participation in healthier behaviours) or productive efficiency (obtaining more health from the same set of inputs). Economists have used a variety of identification strategies to measure the causal effect of education on health behaviours. In the past, schooling concentrated on measure the causal unhealthy behaviours on smoking, but it neglected to measure the causal unhealthy behaviours on drinking alcohol, unhealthy diet and drug mislead. The habit and addition can cause unhealthy behaviour to anyone daily. The marginal utility of current consumption rises with the stock of past consumption to cause habit consumption. So, why the smokers who can not choose to buy any cigarettes to smoke or alcohol to drink easily because whose past buying behaviours are caused to habitual consumption. For example, the first time, an individual consumes the addictive substance, who has a stock of past consumption of zero, but after the individual has been heavy user for sufficiently long to have the maximum stock of past consumption when whose consumption is not only for below the utility who enjoyed during whose first use of additive substance. Hence, this past consumption behaviour has become habitual over longer periods of time.

However, concerning responsiveness of consumption to price, consumption at a point in time is related not only to current prices, but also to past prices. So if permanent price changes can affect demand more than temporary ones because forward-looking persons anticipate and make decisions based on future dynamics in prices. Moreover, the price elasticity of demand for the additive product will be greater in the long run than in the short run and that difference will rise with the level of addictiveness. Specifically, if a rise in price of unhealthy products, such as cigarettes and alcohol that which is expected to cause less consumption in the future. So it becomes optimal to hold a lower quantity of addictive stock, which is achieved by reducing consumption to habitual behaviours.

Rational choice theory assumes that consumers make choices, such that their utility is maximised, subjects to budget constraints. Under rational choice theory, regulation which relaxes budget constraints, increases income, alters relative prices or changes consumer preferences will be effective in changing behaviour. Hence, behavioural economics draws on psychology and behavioural sciences in assessing consumer behaviour. So, social and emotional variables can impact on choice. For example, including simple message which reinforce social norms was found to influence electricity consumption. Such as bad health to smoking or often sit down driving private cars on rest time habits is also good message to reduce consumers who spend too much time to carry on bad health behaving. Under these conditions, some evidence suggests that interventions can be: cost-effective relative to more direct or traditional government intervention, used existing regulatory approaches, targeted in influence and easy to implement. When behavioural economics and rational choice theory provide a useful foundation for policy makers, however both theories also face challenges in their application to regulatory design. So, policy makers ought consider to the specific of markets and market participants when applying any form of consumer theory for purposes of designing and predicting the effects of regulatory policy.

Rational choice theory means consumers rank preferences over all products, makes consumption choices based on these ranking, such their utility is maximized. It is further assumed that individuals rationally pursue their self-interest subject to all economics constraints, such as time, income and capital. Rational choice theory is both positive or negative attitude to any consumer. it seeks to describe how people do behaviour and also how who ought to behave. It will impact on consumer behaviour when it relaxes the consumer's budget constraint, alters prices of products and/or services, e.g. mobile gas price or private car price, smoking price and/or influences a consumer's preferences, such as through information disclosure. Examples of those type of regulation include: financial (dis)incentives, banning or limiting choices, and/or requiring the disclosure of certain information. So, behavioural economics is essentially a series of observations about how people do behaviour in certain situations. It is therefore purely positive. For example, why consumers like to choose to smoke, although who know smoking has bad influence to whose health or why consumers like often drive private cars on rest or relax time on Sunday or Saturday or holiday, although who know who need to pay much gas, even who will lose time to do sport and it is tired to them to drive their private cars often.

Rational choice theory indicates any consumer needs to understand all prices, including opportunity costs, preferences and constraints to make comparison to decide whether who will choose to buy the product or enjoy the service. Could behavioural economics help improve diet quality for nutrition to raise any consumer health? Recognizing that consumption choices are determined by factors other than prices, income and information for consumers' food choices. How to make food choices that promote health and prevent disease. Food manufacturers and marketers have discovered that certain psychological cues, such as packaging and presentation are efficient ways to increase consumption of their products. Could similar marketing approaches be used in public health efforts to improve diet quality and reduce body weight. So, improving diet quality among any nutrition program has the potential to guide food choices at a critical time, when a child's dietary preferences are being defined. For example, letting students preselect menu options to school lunch or school breakfast programs or giving food stamp participants the options to pre order groceries by telephone or online may improve the healthfulness of their food students with parents or guardians could specify purchased with prepaid cards. So, students will consume to select using prepayment (fixed costs), those school nutrition dietary preference often then choice that can be purchased only with cash (variable costs). Hence, this consumption behaviour will influence any student to choose to consume to buy any school breakfast or lunch to eat from dietary preference program by using prepayment prepaid cost purchase method more easily. Because this prepaid card method will cause these students choose to consume school breakfast or lunch habitually more than every time cash payment method in school.

However, the most successful public health programs are based on an understanding of health behaviour and how which can occur. Therefore, interventions to improve health behaviour can be best designed with an understanding of relevant theories of behaviour change and the ability to use than skill. So, development and implementation and evaluation of public health and health behaviour promotion needs to follow theories and key concepts and summarize the evidence about who use of theory in health behaviour research. A theory is a set of interrelated concepts, definitions that explains or predicts events or situations by specifying relations among variables. Theories can guide the health behaviour research to understand why people do or do not practize health promoting behaviours, helping identify what information is need to design and effective intervention strategy and providing insight into how to design a health behaviour program. It has two types of theory, explanatory theory and change theory. For example, understanding why employee smokes is one step toward a successful effort, but even the least explanations won't e enough by themselves to fully guide change to improve health. Both explanatory and change theories can understand the social determinants of health behaviour. Many social cultural and economic factors contribute to the development, maintenance and change of health behaviour patterns. For another example, employees may bring food with the from home or buy food form workplace, cafeterias and vending machines. Their consumption choices are influenced by personal preferences, habits, nutrition information, availability, cost and placement among other things. The choice process is complex and determined not only by multiple factors, but by factors at multiple. Today, no single theory or conceptual framework dominates research or practice in health promotion and education. For example, lifestyle behaviours, such as sexual risk behaviours and injury prevention, the sexual behavioural players who believe about whether or not who are not at risk for a disease or health problem and their perceptions of the benefits of taking action to avoid it, influence their readiness to take action. So predicting health behaviour changing is needed readiness to change or stage of change has been examined in health behaviour research and found useful in explaining and predicting changes for a variety of behaviours, including smoking, physical activity, e.g. householder families often spend time to drive private car to relax and reduce time to do health sport activities.

Labor economy indicates factors of production uses to create products or services, which are not themselves significantly consumed in the production process. The method to create human capital can be categorized into two types. The first is to utilize human as labor force in the classical economic perspective. It means input of labor force is as other production factors, such as financial capital, land machinery and labor hours. Labor capital includes the reading of human as creator who frames knowledge skills, competency and experience originated by continuously connecting between self and environment. Microeconomic model shows that education investment for workers significantly affects whose productivity in the workplace. Education can raise to improve workers productivity. Because it is difficult that human capital itself independently contributes to individual development and national economy growth. In fact, it is necessary to link between human capital and economic preference should be considered within a social and political context to precisely measure the human capital. So human capital is one of important factors for a national economic growth. The production oriented perspective of human capital shows to human capital is as a fundamental source of economic productivity.

Many employers prefer to high productive individuals to improve productivity in the internal labor market by the increasing of productivity in the workplace from internal training to raise old or current workers' skill and knowledge in companies. What is labor surplus mean? Labor surplus exists in the sense that a substantial portion of labor force contributes less to output than it requires, i.e. its marginal product falls below surplus designation than arises from the fact that if such workers were reallocated to enhance the total output of the system. For example, agricultural sectors concentrated especially in subsistence agriculture, characterized by family farm, i.e. excluding planation agricultural which consists of profit maximizing, able to hire or fire workers easily. Surplus labor makes its appearance in the owner-operated extended family networks. The company income or output shares are determined via bargaining in relative to through not necessarily equal to the average rather than the marginal product of labor. Large determination is thus based on a sharing principle, a function of the fact that when high man/land rates are part of the initial conditions low marginal productivity workers can't dismissed or otherwise eliminated. Hence, labor surplus phenomenon will raise unemployed and unfair and unreasonable treatment to the job seekers in labor market because employers only concern family relationship business culture and who only feel the old or current workers who have much effort productivity to compare to other job seekers from labor market. I think who are doing unethical behavior not to give chance to employ any other job seekers to fill their internal job positions, due to they only believe their old or current workers working experience and skills must have more effort to be promoted to higher positions in their companies. So, labor surplus economy will raise unemployment ratio and many labor market of proficient and skillful and knowledgeable owned job seekers who can not get more job opportunities if employers only like to do family relationship workplace culture to protect whose current or old labors benefits only. So, these family relationship employers can not raise productivity and also increasing employment ratio in society if who still do not give chance to accept to employ outside job seeker to assist whose business development for long term.

However, labor market policies succeed or fail at least concerning for behavioral response. Insight from behavioral economics, hence consequences for the design and function of labor market policies. For example, the human costs of labor market have rarely been clearer at the value of public policies, such as unemployment insurance and job training programs that assist workers in managing, gaining new skills and navigating the labor of joblessness have been apparent in most major economics in recent years. For the design of unemployment insurance with job search requirements intended to minimize worry to incentives to return to work. I think behavioral economy can apply to labor market finds in these areas to solve labor challenges: unemployment insurance, job search assistance and job training. Hence solving labor moral hazard problems in unemployment compensation schemes of unemployed workers not putting in adequate search efforts and setting inefficiently high reservation wages in response to more generous benefits when unemployed. However, economists have noted several advantages to wage loss insurance, such as the ability to better target benefits to those workers who face the most severe consequence of job loss. Although, behavioral economists doesn't change that logic, it does identify additional advantages to wage loss insurance. There behavioral concerns are consistence with the limited impacts on reemployment rates and job search efforts for encourage the unemployed people have more effort to find new jobs during this period of unemployment period if governments can provide temporary wage loss insurance to them. In any country's labor market, it has supply two sides, the factors affect the decision of an individual. On the supply side, factors include working nature, career path top choose a particular job, requiring education and on the job training, providing effort in particular job. Also, on the demand side, factors that affect the decision of an individual firm factors include: how the firm hires and fires workers, how it offer jobs with different characteristics, how it discriminate among different workers and how it chooses particular compensation policies and to offer different career paths to workers. So, behavioral economist is the combination of psychology and economic that investigates what happens in markets in which some of the agents display human limitations. Does some combination of market formed, learning and evolution these human qualities irrelevant? Because of limits of perfect agents (human) survive and influence what outcomes. Surely, all of economic is meant to be about the behavior of economic agents be whose firms or consumers, suppliers or demanders, bankers or farmers. So what is behavioral economic and how does it differ from other economic? Do only the rational agents survive? Do the workings of markets at least render the actions of rational irrelevant? So, what the decision if it was a mistake to do any rational calculation before the consumer does any decision. So, it seems behavioral economy and psychology has close relationship. It means that human psychology will influence whose decision how to do any economic activities. For example, public economic is the study of how government economic is the study of how government policies influence economic market. Hence, economic analysis is part of the decision making process in any organizations or individuals.

To conclude labour economy and behavioural economy has different functions. Behavioural economy has close relationship to psychology research. Behavioural economists need to find what causes the consumer why who choose to do whose behaviour or how to predict the consumer avoids to do whose behaviour. Otherwise, labour economists need to concern how to assist the employer to avoid whose employees who feel unfair or unreasonable moral behaviour from whose employer to reduce low productivity caused. Hence, labour economy concerns on individual benefit more than public benefit. Otherwise, behavioural economy concerns on public benefit more than individual benefit. Labour economy concerns on raising individual productivity. Otherwise, behavioural economy concerns on change individual or public habit of behaviour to raise sale.

Bibliography

Roberston, R. (1992), Globalization, Social Theory and

How utility maximization, equilibrium and efficiency concepts influence employee's individual behavior

At the core of behavioral economics is used psychology of economics analysis to improve economics on its own terms generating theoretical insights, making better prediction of field phenomena, and suggesting better policy. It rejects economic theories based on utility maximization, equilibrium and efficiency. It is useful because it provides economists with a theoretical framework that can be applied to almost any form of economic (and even non-economic) behavior.

Simpifying much assumption that are not central to the economic theory. For example, there is nothing in core theory that specifies that people should not care about fairness, that they should weight risky outcomes in a linear fashion, or that they must discount the future at a constant rate. Other assumption simply acknowledge human limits on computational power and self-interest. These assumptions can be considered procedurally rational because human needs to solve problems that are often so complex that who can't be solved exactly by even modern computer technology.

Theories in behavioral economics should be judged by reality, generality and tractability concepts. We share the positivist view that the ultimate test of a theory is the accuracy of its predictions. But we also believe that better predictions are likely to result from theories with more realistic assumptions. In psychology, such as connectionist models that capture some of the essential features of neural functioning, which are based on utility maximization, yet are reaching the point where they are able to predict many judgemental and behavioral phenomena. Contrary to the positivistic view, however,
we believe that predictions of feelings.

Most of the ideas in behavioral economics are not new. When economics first became identified as a distinct field of study, psychology didn't exist as a discipline. For example, "invisible hand" and "the wealth of Nations" which belong to theory to moral sentiments, which laid out psychological principles of individual behavior that are arguably as profound as whose economic observations. Another example, such as a simple model of social utility means that one person's utility was affected by another person's payoff. However, the rejection of academic psychology by economists, which constructed an account of economic behavior built up from assumptions about the nature-that is, the psychology of homo-economicus. Nowadays, economists hoped their discipline could be like a natural science. But psychology was not very scientific. The economists thought it provided too unsteady a foundation for economics, who make assumption to utility led to a movement to the psychology from economics. In the early part of the 20th century, economists still included rich speculations about

how people feel and think about economic choices generally. However, later economists are very much appealed to psychological insights, but by the middle of the century discussions of psychology had largely disappeared. Throughout the second half of the century, many criticisms of the positivistic perspective took place in both economics and psychology. The economists of the time had less disagreement with psychology with psychology than they realized. They assume without foundation that behavior always aims at the goal of maximum pleasure and minimum pain; but behavior is not goal-oriented. Also the economists of the time believed false conclusions are drawn from false psychological assumptions. The importance of psychological measures and bounds on rationality. These commentators attracted attention, but did not alter the fundamental direction of economics. One development was the rapid acceptance by economists of the expected utility and discounted utility models which are making decision under uncertainty and choice, respectively. Whereas the assumptions and implications of utility analysis are rather flexible, and the expected utility and discounted utility models have numerous precise and testable implications. As a result, they provided some of the first "hand targets" for critics of the standard theory.

As economists began to accept counterexamples that could be not be permanently ignored, developments in psychology identified promising directions for new theory.

Beginning around 1960 year, psychology became dominated by the brain as an information-processing device replacing the behaviorist conception of the brain as a stimulus-response machine. The information-processing permitted a fresh study of neglected topics like memory, problem solving and decision making. These new topics were more obviously relevant to the conception of utility maximization than behaviorism had appeared to be. However, psychologists began to use economic models as a benchmark against which to constrast their psychological models. Early research in behavioral have followed. First, identify assumption or models that are used by economists, who expected utility and discounted utility. Second, the assumption or model is a rule out alternative explanations (such as subjects' confusion or transactions costs). And third, the assumption or model creates alternative theories that generalize existing models. The fourth step is to construct economic models of behavior using the behavioral assumptions to test them from the third step. This final step of economic models of behavior has only been taken more recently to apply.

Costs and benefits analysis concept measures consumer's individual or employee's individual behavior

The methods in behavioral economics are the same as those in other areas of economies. In fact, behavioral economics relied heavily on evidence generated by experiments. More recently, however, behavioral economists have moved beyond experimentation and the full range of methods are employed by economists. The experiements played a large role in the initial phase of behavioral economics because experimental control is exceptionally helpful for distinguishing behavioral explanations from standard ones. Suppose we observed this phenomenon in these any one of cares, in the form of failures of legal cases to settle before trial, costly divorce proceedings, and labor strikes. They are phenomenons of human‘ behaviours are caused by costs and benefits measurement of result. Also, behavioural economy would be difficult to tell whether rejection of offers was the result of reputation-building in repeated games, agency problems (between clients and lawyers), confusion, or an expression of distaste for being treated unfairly. However, in these game experiments of failures of legal cases to settle before trial, costly divorce proceedings, and labor strikes. The first three of these explanations are ruled out because the experiments are played once, have no agents, and are simple enough to rule out confusion. Thus, the experimental data clearly establish that subjects are expressing concern for fairness. Other experiments have been useful for testing whether judgment errors which individuals commonly make in psychology experiments also affect prices and quantities in markets. The lab is especially useful for these studies because individual and market-level data can be observed. Although behavioral economists relied on experimental data, however, behavioral economics subject is seen as a very different method from experimental economics. As noted, behavioral economists are methodological profession. They define themselves, not on the basis of the research methods that who employ, but rather their application of psychological insights to economics. Experimental economists, on the other hand, define themselves on the basis of use of experimentation which is as a research tool. Also, economists have made a major investment in developing experimental methods that are suitable for addressing economic issues, and have achieving among themselves on a number of important issues. For example, experimental economists often make instructions and software available for precise replication, and raw data are typically shared for reanalysis. Experimental economists also insist on paying performance-based. However, experimental economists have also developed rules that many behavioral economists are likely to find excessively . For example, experimental economists rarely collect data like demographics, self-reports, reponse times and other cognitive measure which behavioral economists have found useful. Descriptions of the experimental environment are usually abstract rather than which are carried on experiment in the outside world because economic theory rarely makes a prediction about how a happen would matter, and experimenters are concerned about losing control over incentives if choosing strategies with certain labels is appealing because of the labels themselves.

Finally, economic experiments also typically use "stationary replication", in which the same task is repeated over and over in each period. Data from the last few periods of the experiment are typically used to draw conclusions about equilibrium behavior outside the lab. When economists believe that examining behavior after it is of great interest, it is also obvious that many important aspects of economic life are like the first few periods of an experiment rather than the last. Supposing if we need to make decision of marriage, educational decisions, and saving for retirement, or the purchase of large durables like houses, sailboats, can cars, which happen just a few times in a person's life, a focus on behavior is clearly not warranted. All said, the focus on psychological realism and economic applicability of research promoted by the behavioral-economics perspective suggests the usefullness research outside the lab and of a broader range of approaches to laboratory research. So, economists realize that who have ideal opportunity to learn by trial-and-error, in a stationary environment, and uses the opportunity to learn how to carry on experimenting any psychology and behavioral researches.

The field of behavioral decision research, on which behavioral economics has drawn more than any other subfield of psychology, typically classifies research into two categories: judgement and choice. Judgement research deals with the processes people use to estimate probabilities. Choice deals with the processes people use to select among actions, considering of any relevant judgements who may have made. Everyday, we need to make probable judements. Due to judging the likelihood of events is central to economic life. For example: Will you lose your job in a poor economic environment? Will you be able to find another house you like as much as the one you must bid for right away? Will the government raise interest rates? Will a merger strategy increase profits? These questions are answered by some process of judging likelihood. The standard principles used in economic to model probability judgement in economic are concepts of statistical sampling, which are concerned probabilities in the face of new evidence. However, it requires a separation between previously judged probabilities and evaluations of new evidence. However, people often overestimate the probability who previously attached to events which later happened. This leads to "secondguessing". For example, Monday morning quarterbacking and may be partly responsible for lawsuits against stockbrokers who lost money for their clients. (The clients think the brokers should have known). For example, anybody has tried to learn from a computer manual has seen the curse of knowledge in action. Another example for making probability judgements is called "representativeness": People judge conditional probabilities like P(hypothesis /data) or P(example/class) by how well the data represents the hypothesis or the example represents the class. Representativeness is an economical shortcut that delivers reasonable judgements with minimal effort in many cases. For example, in judging whether a certain student described in a profile is, say, a psychology major or computer science major, the student decides how well the profile matches the psychology or computer science career to the student generally.

Many studies show how this sort of feature-matching can lead people to underweigh the "base rate", in this example, the overall frequency of the two majors. Another byproduct of representativeness is the "law of small numbers": Small samples are though to represent the properties of the statistical process that generated them (as if the law of large numbers, which guarantees that a large sample of independent draws does represent the process, is in a hurry to work). If a baseball player get hits 30% of his times at bat, but is 0 for 4 , so far in a particular game, then he is "due" for a hit in his next at bat in this game, so that this game's hitting profile will more closely represent his overall ability. Field and experimental studies with basketball shooting and betting on games that people believe that there is positive attitude that players experience the "hot hand", when there is no evidence that such an effect exists. For example, judgements of the fairness or non misleading or reasonable of clients' financial report to accounting auditors, consumers buying products and classroom negotiation. It is important to judge whether it is both a good attitude and bad attitude. A good attitude provides fast, close to optimal, answers when time or capabilities are limited, but it also needs logical principles and leads to situations. So, optimal is largely a critique (a reasonable one) of the later applied research. Assume that people misspecify a set of hypotheses, or encode new evidence incorrectly. For example, assuming that people believe hypothesis A is more likely than B will never encode pro-A evidence mistakenly, but will sometimes encode pro-B evidence as being supportive. For another example, investors will think there is wide variation in skill of, say, mutual-fund managers, even if there is no variation at all. (A manager who does well several years is a surprise if performance is mistakenly thought due to nonreplacement, so concluding that the manager must be really good.) A question concerns stock market, such as: Overreacts in the long term. In their model, earnings follow a random walk but investors believe, mistakenly, that earnings have positive attitude. After one or two periods of good earnings, the stock market can not be confident that exists and hence expects, but since earnings are really a random walk, the stock market is too pessimistic and is underreacting to good earnings news. After a good earnings, however, the stock market believes many investors are increasing. Since, it is not the stock market is too optimistic and overreact. For another example, valuable consumer products (A $100 wireless keyboard, a fancy computer mouse, bottles of wine, and a box of chocolate) are sold to postgraduate (MBA) business students. The students were presented with a product and asked whether who would buy it for a price equal to the last two digits of their own social security number (a roughly random identification number required to obtain work in the United States) converted into a dollar figure, e.g. , if the last digits were 99, then the postgraduate business students will accept the hypothetical price was $99 to buy any of it for a price to the last two digits of their own social security number . After giving a yes/no response to the question. Would you pay $99? subjects were asked to state the most who would pay (using a procedure that gives people an incentive to say what who really would pay). Although subjects were reminded that the social security number is essentially random, those with high numbers were willing to pay more for the products. However, many studies have also shown that the method used to elicit preferences can have dramatic consequences. Nevertheless, when required to make an economic decisions-to-choose a brand of toothpaste, a car, a job, or how to invest, people do make some kind of decision. Behavioral economists refer to the process by which people make choices with ill defined preferences as "constructing preferences".

However, in classical consumer theory, preferences among different commodities are assumed to be invariant with respect to an individual's current consumption. Specifically, people seem to dislike losing commodities from their consumption much more than they like gaining other commodities. For example, the research of "contingent valuation" studies that attempt to establish the dollar value of products which are not routinely trades. Contingent valuation is often used to do government cost-benefit analysis or establish legal penalties from environment damage. These surveys typically show very large differences between buying prices (e.g. paying to clean up oil of beaches) and selling prices (e.g. having to be paid to allow beaches to be ruined).

Nowadays, a quarter of the wealth in the USA has more interesting opportunities to do behavioral economies. They find that motivated sellers should regard the price who paid as a sunk cost and choose at a nominal loss from the purchase price. Sellers' listing prices and subsequent selling behavior reflects to nominal losses. There are some cases in which no effect would be expected, such as when products are purchased for resale rather than for utilization. For example, Do art or antique dealers like with pieces who buy to resell? What about surrogate mothers who agree to bear a child for a price paid in advance? However, evidence on the degree of commercial attachment is mixed. Reference points can also serve as social focal points for judging performance. For an interesting example from corporate finance. In general, when managers whose firms face possible losses (or declines from a previous year's earnings) are very reluctant to report small losses. As a result, the distribution of actual losses and gains show a very large at zero, and hardly any small reported losses (compared to the number of small gains). A manager who does not have the skill to shift accounting profits to erase a potential loss (i.e. has some earnings in his pocket.) is considered a poor manager. It seems that the bad performance manager whose behavior is bad to mislead public to believe his firm have better performance in this year. Hence, in the mental accounting view, people set up mental accounts for outcomes which are psychologically separate, much as financial accountants lump expenses and revenues into separated accounts to guide managerial attention. Otherwise, mental accounting stands in opposition to the standard view in economics that it predicts, accurately , that people will spend money coming from different sources in different ways. So, a generalization of the notion of mental accounting is the concept of "choice bracket" , which refers to the fashion in which people make decisions narrowly, in either a piece meal fashion, or boardly, i.e. taking account of interdependencies between decisions. For example, when making many separate choices between products, consumers tend to choose more diversity when the choices are bracketed broadly than when they are bracketed narrowly.

Explanation what are of Preferences over risky and uncertain outcomes of individual behavior economic theories.

The expected utility (EU) hypothesis explains that the utility of a risky distribution of outcomes (says, monetary payoffs) is a probability weighted average of the outcome utilities. It follows logically from apparently reasons. Most notably the independence (or " cancellation") choice. The indepence choice says that if you are comparing two gambles, you should cancel events which lead to the same consequence with the same probability, your choice should be independent of those utility also simplifies matters because a person's taste for risky money distributions can be fully captured by the share of the utility function for money.

However, many studies document predictive failures of expected utility in simple situations in which subjects can earn substantial sums of money from their choices. Some of these new theories alter the way in which probabilities are weighted, but preserve a "betweenness" property which says that if A is preferred to B, then any probabilistic gamble between them must be preferred to B, but dispreferred to A (i.e. the gambles like "between" A and B in preference). Other new theories suggest that probability weights are "rank-dependent", outcomes are first ranked, then their probabilities are weighted in a way which is sensitive to how who rank within the gamble that is being considered. For example, if a person is attitude towards gambles really came from the utility of wealth function, even large gains in wealth would not tempt who to risk $50 or $100 losses, if who really dislikes losing $10 more than who likes gaining $11 at every level of wealth. For example, linear probability weighting in expected utility (EU) works reasonably well except when outcome probabilities are very low or high. But low-probability events are important in the economy in the form of "gambles" with positive (lottery tickets and also risky business ventures in biotechnology and pharmaceuticals) and high risk compensation events which required large insurance industries. Another theory example, such as prospect theory is experimental choices more accurately than (EU) because it gets the psychological of judgement and choice right. It consists of two main components, a probability weighting function, and a "value function" which replaces the utility function of (EU). The weighting function P(P) combines two elements: (1) The level of probability weight is a way of expressing risk tastes (if you hate to gamble, you will place low weight on any chance of winning anything) and (2) P(P) captures how sensitive people are to differences in probabilities. If people are move sensitive in the neighborhoods of possibility and certainty. i.e. changes in probability near zero and 1, then their P(P) curve will overweight low probabilities and underweight high ones. For another theory example, such as technical motivation for "rank dependent" theories, ranking outcomes, than weighting their probabilities is that when separate probabilities are weighted, it is easy to construct examples in which people will be dominance by choosing a "dominated" gamble A which has a lower chance of winning at each possible outcome amount, compared to the higher chance of winning the same outcome amount for a dominant gamble B. If people rarely choose such dominated gambles, who are acting as if who are weighting the differences in probabilities which is the essence of the rank dependent approaches. So, new information can help any decision maker to feel better to make better decisions. These theories effect may explain demand for information in settings like medicine or personal finance, where new information usually does not change choice, but relieves anxiety people have from knowing there is something who could know but don’t. However, the planning problem for economic agents who would like to behave in fashion and discussed the important time discounting for choice. Most big decisions, e.g. savings, educational investments, labor supply, health and diet, crime and drug etc. decisions use have costs and benefits which occur at different point in time. Thus, time discounting is basically standard time discounting plus an immediacy effect, a decision discounts delays in equally at all moments except the current one, caring differently about well being. This functional form provides one sample and powerful model of the taste to individual to make right or reasonable behavior economic decision. However, most analyses of choice assume that people integrate new consumption with planned consumption. It is infeasible and perhaps for this reason, descriptively inaccurate. When people make decisions about new sequences of payments or consumption, they tend to evaluate them in isolation, e.g. treating negative outcomes as losses, rather than as reductions to their existing money flows or consumption plans.

How to decide fairness and social preferences. The assumption that people maximize their own wealth and other personal material goals just self-interest is a correct simplification that is often useful in economics. However, people may sometimes choose to spend their wealth to punish others who have harmed them, reward whose, so who have helped, or to make outcomes more fair. Just as understanding demand for products requires specific utility function, the key to understanding this sort of social preferences is a specification of social utility which can explain many types of date with a single function.

Behavioral economy can also use to assist firms to choose right behavior to decide to do any matters. I show hypothesis to establish any reference level of consumer surplus and product profit. Both sides are entitled to any firm's levels of profit, so price changes which threaten any matter are considered unfair. So raising any product price, it will reduce consumer surplus and is considered unfair. But the cost of a firm's inputs rises, subjects said it was fair to raise prices. Because not raising prices would reduce the firm's profit (compared to the reference profit). Everyday observation that firms don't change prices and wages as frequently commonly. For example, when the fourth hary potter story book was released in summer 2000 year, most stores were allocated a small number of books that were pre-sold in advance. Why not raise prices or auction the books off? It is possible that it concerned about customer goodwill and excess demand to cause book stores limit such book price increases. Offended consumers are often able to affect firm behavior by media attention or provoking legislation. For example, scalping tickets for populr sports and entertainment events (resulting them at a large premium over the printed ticket price) is constrained by law in most countries. For example, some countries have "anti-laws" penalizing sellers who take advantage of shortages of water, fuel and other necessities by raising prices after natural disasters. So, the countries' governments can protect which citizen benefits to balance the natural resource supply and demand to sell in the reasonable price fairly after the natural disaster occurrence.

A few years ago, responding to public anger at rising CEO salaries when the economy was being restructured through downsizing and many workers lost their jobs. Otherwise, some countries passed a law prohibiting firms from deducting CEO salaries for tax purposes beyonded $1 million a year. because the countries need to earn much tax income from these high salary CEO income every year. So, explaining why these laws and regulations come from is one example of now economics might be used to expand the scope of law and behavioral economic relationship.

What is behavioral game theory?

Game theory has rapidly become an important foundation for many areas of economic theory, such as bargaining in decentralized markets, contracting and organizational structure. The descriptive accuracy of game theory in these application can be questioned because equilibrium predictions often assume strategic reasoning and direct field tests are difficult. In fact, behavioral game theory uses any experimental evidence and psychological research to generalize the standard assumptions of game theory. One component of behavioral game theory is a theory of social preferences for allocations of money to oneself and others. Another component is a theory of how people choose in one shot games or in the first period of a repeated game. For example, in share buying and selling market, shareholders shall buy or sell shares from their judgement in the economic cycle market everyday. So share investment is seemed as allocation of game to these shareholders. Also, shareholders whose mind can influence whose psychological behavior to decide how to invest whose shares in their share investment economic activities. The component of behavioral game theory can include a model of learning to either individual or a population. Also, game theory is one area of economy in which serious attention has been paid to the process by which can equilibrium comes about. Many learning theories have been proposed and carefully tested with experimental data. Theories about population never predict as well as theories of individual learning through who are useful for other purposes. So, behavioral game theory can be applied to these complex environments. e.g. consumer supermarket purchase, share market etc. How to apply behavioral game theory to macroeconomics and saving aspect? Many concepts in macroeconomic probably have a behavioral style that could be influenced by research in psychology. For example, it is common to assume that prices and wages are in nominal terms, which has important implications for macroeconomic behavoir. Behavioral economics suggests some ideas for among consumers and workers, perhaps it is influenced by workers' concern for fairness. An important model in macroeconomics is the life cycle model of savings or permanent income hypothesis. This theory assumes that people make a guess about their lifetime earnings profile, and plan their lifetime earnings profile, and plan their savings and consumption in each period has diminishing marginal utility; and preferences for consumptions streams are time-separable (i.e. overall utility is the sum of the discounted utility of consumption in each separate period). The theory also assumes people lump together different types income when they guess how much money who will have (i.e. different sources of wealth are different). So, why many young people won't spend too much money for unnecessary expenditure, e.g. entertainment easily. Because who plan to save for their retirement in the future.

A behavioral life cycle theory of savings in which different sources of income are kept track of in different mental accounts. Mental accounts can reflect natural perceptual or cogitive divisions. For example, it is possible to add up the travellers' paycheck and dollar value of whose frequent flyer miles, but it is simply unnatural to do so. It is important to note that many key implications of the life-cycle hypothesis have never been well supported (e.g. consumption is far more closely related to current income than it should be according to theory. However, predictions can be improved by introducing utility functions with habit formation in which utility in a current depends on the reference point of previous consumption, and by more carefully accounting for uncertaining about future income. So, mental accounting is only one of several behavioral approaches that may prove useful. Economics is money illusion, it is the tendency to make decisions based on nominal quantities rather than converting those figures into real terms by adjusting for inflation. Money illusion seems to be pervasive in some domains. So, it appears that employees don't seem to mind if their real wage falls as long as their nominal wages doesn't fall. Labor macroeconomics is involuntary unemployment. Why can some people not find work beyond of switching jobs, or a natural rate of unemployment? A popular account of unemployment pushs that wages are deliberately paid above the market clearly level, which creates an excess supply of workers and hence unemployment. But why are wages too high ? As efficiency wage theory shows that paying workers more than who deserve is necessary to ensure that who have something to lose if they are unemployed, which motivates them to work hand and economizes on monitoring. Another viewpoint indicates that employer and worker is such as into a gift exchange relationship. Employers pay more than who have to as a gift and workers repay the gift by working harder than necessary. They show how gift exchange can be an equilibrium and show some of its macroeconomic implications. In labor economics, gift exchange is clearly evident of experimental labor markets. In practical working environment, firms offer wages; workers who take the jobs than choose a level of effort, which is costly to the workers and valuable to the firms. For example, firms and workers can enforce wages, but not effort levels. Since workers and firms are matched for just one period, and do not learn each other's identities, there is no way for either side to build reputations or for firms to punish workers who chose low effort. However, self interested workers should shirk, and firms should anticipate that and pay a low wage. In fact, firms deliberately pay high wages as gifts and workers choose higher effort levels when they take higher wage jobs. It seems that it has strong relationship between wages and effort is stable over time. For example, standard life-cycle theory assumes that if people can borrow they should prefer wage profiles which maximize the present value of lifetime wages. Holding total wage payments constant, and assuming a positive real rate of interest, present value maximization implies that workers should prefer declining wage profiles over increasing ones. However, in fact, most wages profiles are clearly rising over time which is such as a phenomenon. Rather, workers derive utility from positive changes in consumption, but have self-control problems. That would prevent them from positive changes in consumption, but have self-control problems that would prevent them from saving for later consumption of wages were more front-loaded in the life cycle. In addition, workers seem to derive positive utility from increasing wage profiles, it is perhaps because rising wages are a source of self-esteem and the desire for increasing payments is much weaker for non wage income. The standard life-cycle of labor supply also implies that workers should substitute labor and leisure based on the wage rate who face and the value who place on leisure at different points in time. If wage fluctuations are temporary workers should work long hours when wages are high and short hours when wages are low. However, because changes in wages are often persisting and because work hours are generally fixed in the short-run. So, it is difficult to tell whether workers are substituting. For example, taxi drivers who target daily will drive longer hours on low income days and guit early on high income days. This behavior is exactly the opposite of substitution. Also inexperienced taxi drivers support the daily targeting prediction. But experienced taxi drivers don't have negative elasiticies, either because target minded drivers earn less and self select or taxi drivers learn over time to substitute rather than target. Perhaps the simplest prediction of labor economics is that the supply of labor should be upward sloping in response to a increase in wage.

In finance, stantard equilibrium models of asset pricing assume that investors only care about asset risks if who affect marginal publicly available information to forecast stock returns as accurately as possible the efficient markets hypothesis. When those hypotheses do make some accurate predictions and some investors in assets have limited rationality of behavioral finance. Also, in share stock market, it is common, shareholders should not want to trade with them, but the volume of stock market transaction is large. So, it presents data on individual trading behavior which suggests that the extremely high volume may be driven, in part, by overconfidence on the part of investors. For example, property agent's individual behavior is similar to share agent's individual behavior. In the economy view, property agent bases a list price for a house on the selling prices of nearly houses that is similar ("comparables"). Every nearest neighbour techniques bases on similarity is also used in credit scoring and other kinds of evaluations. Also, one firm whose every share sale on the selling price is comparable to its similar firms whose every share price in its same business industry. The shareholder will evaluate whose every share issued sale price in the stock (share) market. Otherwise, in behavioral economy view, for example, property or share buyer who has risky choice to decide to buy in the property or share market. It is a process of comparing the similarity of the probabilities and outcomes in two gambles and choosing on dimensions which are dissimilar.

As we mentioned above, behavioral economics simply includes an interest in psychology. In fact, we believe that many familiar economic distinctions do have a lot of behavioral content, they are implicitly behavioral, and could surely benefit from more explicit ties to psychological ideas and data. However, some people do not feel psychology and economy which have close relationship. Such as, substantial debate is ongoing in psychology about whether knowing the precise details of how the brain carries out computations is necessary to understand functions and mechanisms of driving car skill at higher levels, (knowing the mechanical details of how a car works may not be necessary to turn the key and drive it). Most psychology experiments use indirect measures like response times, error self reports and natural experiments, due to brain has been fairly successful in codifying what we know about thinking, but pressimists think brain scan studies won't add much. The optimists think the new tools will lead to some discoveries. Another couple is the distinction between short run and long run price elasticity which concerns behavioral economy. In fact, economy needs have theories concepts to support any evidence to prove any matter has happened. Concerning short run and long run price elasticity cause and effort issue, with a casual suggestion that the run is the time it takes for markets to adjust, or for consumers to learn new prices, after a demand or supply stock. Adjustment costs undoubtedly have technical and social component, but probably also have some behavioral factors influence in the form of gradual adaption to loss and learning.

Another macroeconomic model which can be interpreted as implicitly behavioral is that business cycles can emerge if it is not general price inflation, so why the consumers shall not decide to buy this kind of product in the competitive market. For example, risky choice is as a process of comparing the similarity of the probabilities and outcomes in two gambles, and choosing on dimensions which are dissimilar. Behavioral economic simply includes an interest in psychology. In fact, we believe that many familiar economic distinctions do have a lot of behavioral content, they are implicitly behavioral and could surely benefit from more explicit ties to psychological ideas and data. However, some people do not feel psychology and economy which have close relationship. Such as psychology is about whether knowing the precise details of how the brain carries out computations is necessary to understand functions and mechanisms at higher levels. (knowing the mechanical details of how a car works may not necessary to turn the key and drive it.) Most psychology experiments use indirect measures like response times, error rates, self reports and natural experiments due to brain has been fairly successful in codifying what we know about thinking. However, pessimists think brain scan studies won't add much. The optimists think the new tools will lead to some discoveries and the potential is great that they cannot be ignored. However, economy needs have theories or concepts to support evidence to prove why any matters had happened. An example, is the distinction between short term and long term price elasticity. This distinction, mentions between of them, with a casual suggestion that long run is the time it takes for markets to adjust, or for consumers to learn new prices, after a demand or supply shock. Adjustment costs undoubtedly have technical and social components, but probably also have some behavioral factors influence in the form of gradual adaption to loss and learning.

However, organizational behavioral theory concerns that organizatonal contracting are shot through with implicitly behavioral economics. Some economists motivate the incompleteness of contracts as a consequence of rationality in foreseeing the future, but do not tie the research directly to work on memory and imagination. For example, agency theory begins with the presumption that there is some activity the agent doesn't like to do. Why markets are better at making dramatic changes than managers influence cost. So, influence costs are the costs managers preform for projects who like or personally benefit from like promotion or raises. A lot of influence costs are undoubtedly inflated by optimistic, each division manager really does think their division desperately needs funds and social comparison of pay and benefits. Otherwise, why are salaries kept so secret? In all these cases, conventional economic behavior has deeper psychological questions of where adjustment costs, effort and influence costs come from. So, it beings these questions: Could these phenomena surely produce surprising testable prediction? Is psychology regularity an assumption or a conclusion?

Behavioral economics generally begins with assumption rooted in psychological regularity and asks what follows from those assumptions. An alternative approach is to work backward, regarding a psychological regularity as a conclusion that must be proved an explanation that must be derived from deeper assumption before we fully understand and accept it. The alternative approach is caused by a fashionable new direction in economic theory and psychology too, which is to explain human behavior as the product of evolution. However, we may not believe that behavior of intelligent, modern people lived in socialization and cultural influence can only be understood by guessing what their lives were like and how their brains might have adapted generally. There are other models that treat psychological regularity as a conclusion to be proved rather than an assumption to be used. Such models usually begin with an observed regularity. Economists have for deriving behavior from first principles and rationalizing apparent irrationality. Theories of this sort are useful behavioral economics and what fresh predictions do they make. However, critics have pointed out that behavioral economics is not a unified theory, but is instead a collection of tools and ideas. This is true. However, some economists believe that economic models do not derive much predictive power from the single tool of utility maximization. The goal of behavioral economic is to develop better tools that, in some cases, can do both jobs at once. Economists like to point out the natural division of labor between scientific disciplines: Psychologists should concern to individual minds, and economists to behavior in games, markets, and economies. But the division of labor is only efficient if there is effective coordinaton, and all too often economists fail to conduct intellectual trade with those who have a comparative advantage in understanding individual human behavior. The only question is whether the implicit psychology in economics is good psychology or bad psychology. We think it is simply unwise, and inefficient to do economics without paying some attention to good psychology.

What is the relationship between behavioral economic principle and policy makers or decision makers ?

Behavioral economics theories can also apply to assist any policy makers to make right and reasonable decision in right time. I shall indicate new principles to recommend and I also shall give any psychological cases to explain how policy makers can apply behavioral economic theories to judge how to make their any decision is the most right and the most reasonable.

Behavioral economy is an independent and demonstrates real economic well-being. It aims to improve quality of life by promoting innovative solutions that challenge mainstream thinking on economic, environment and social issues. Also, behavioral economy is different branches of more alternative economies into a form that is useful primarily for policy-makers. I think behavioral economy can be given an aid to policy makers how who use economic tools to the broader policy making community by providing a theoretical behaviour for many policy approaches to be used. The standard economic analysis assumes that humans are rational and behave in a way to maximize their individual self-interest. This rational man assumption indicates a powerful tool for analysis. However, it has many shortfalls that can lead to unrealistic economic analysis and policy-making. Also, I think behavioral economics and psychology has these principles to influence human behaviour. These principles include, such as below:

In common, people do many things by observing others and copying; people are encouraged to continue to do things when they feel other people approve of their behaviour. People do many things without consciously thinking about time. These habits are hard to change. There are cases where money is de-motivating as it undermines people's intrinsic motivation. People want their actions and commitments to be values usually. People put undue weight on recent events and who cann't calculate probabilities well and worry too much about unlikely events and who are strongly influences by how the problem/information is presented to them. People need to feel effective to make a change, even just giving who the incentives and information is not necessarily enough in any environment usually. So policy makers ought concern about these human behavior principles to judge whose behaviors are right or wrong, then who can decide to do any economic activities more reasonable, e.g. decisions of consumption, policies making, investment etc.

In fact, much of our behaviour is strongly influenced by other people's behaviour. Social learning is a process by which we take in the behavior of others to learn how to behave. In more complex situations with which we are unfamiliar, we consciously watch and learn from the behavior of others. For example, when use a new library for the first time. When we mist make a conscious decision on how to behave, our sense of social identity is important, we think: how would other from my group behave in this situation? In situations where there is high social capital. i.e. where there are strong networks between people and a high level of mutual trust, so its seems other people's behaviour and our sense of social identity may be extremely important in influencing our own behavior and policy makers ought need to know how to judge their behaviour whether their behavior is either right and reasonable or wrong and unreasonabe in any learning process of environment. The standard economic theory is tried to explain where people's preferences come from, so it does not take account of the direct influence of the people's behaviour and social norms on our behaviour. The theory assumes we independently know what we want and that our preferences are fixed. This standard theory is very good at explaining short-term decision making. For example, I want green vegetables and choose fruits as they are on special offer, but it cannot explain longer term changes in preferences. I now only choose organic food. Along the same lines the importance of institutions, such as regulations, for example, how people organise markets and the evolution of the whole economi system are not subjects of general economic analysis. This has significant implications for policy design.

In fact, the standard economic theory also assumes that people carry out a full rational analysis of all consumers' available options. This is not what we do; we often just copy the actions of other people. For example, it would require too much effort to look up all the rules when driving in a new country, to find out all the fines/punishments for failing to meet the rules, to work out the probability of being caught and the possible costs, before deciding how to drive there. Instead we just copy other people, and perhaps adjust our behaviour according to the feedback we receive. However, some psychologists indicate to see people how to behave, especically in crises situations and when others are experts. These psychologists have identified that we are open to influence from people in authority or people we like. When we are influenced by authority, an expert, someone with legitimate power to direct our actions, someone who can either reward or punish us. The effects are less likely to be lasting than we are influenced by someone we like.

However, some people's psychological behaviour is similar to economic behaviour to judge to make any decision. For example, why do you wear a seatbelt in your car? Most of us wear seatbelts as it has became normal behaviour, everyone does it. We neither evaluate the likelihood of having an accident, nor the chance of getting caught without our seatbelt on and incurring a fine. The enforcement of seatbelt wearing is now hardly necessary, as it has become a social norm. What does this mean for policy makers? Policy makers focusing only on economic analysis may often devise a system that has an immediate effect. In psychologists view this issue point, knowing that there is a fine for speeding and a high likelihood of getting caught, the driver will probably drive more slowly, but who will drive just as fast one who realise the chance of being caught is low. However, of policy makers can change the social norm, perhaps in this case by encouraging us to frown on others who drive dangerously fast with campaigns against dangerous driving, then less enforcement will be needed after the change. In other words policy makers might want to take preferences as fixed in the short term, but they should consider shifting preferences in the medium term. An example where policy appears to have successfully changes people's preferences in the US and Singapre and Hong Kong is banning smoking in public places. This change appears to reduce the social proof of the amount people smoke in private places and public places both also. It seems that government policies can influence the decreasing numbers of consumers require to buy cigeratte to smoke habitually, due to fine and punishment is regulated to be ban effectively. Such daily routines quickly became habits. Even when we consciously think about what we do, it can be difficult to change our behaviour. Perhaps I think it is a good idea for people to use public transport, but I do not know where the bus stop is or when the bus runs. I think to use private car to drive to work place is more preference choice. The reward feeling , my journey by car was easy and free to reinforce my old bad habit. Psychologists theories on changing habits generally involve raising it to a conscious level where we can consider the merits of alternative behaviour. This is followed by adopting the new behaviour, which, with time, becomes frozen as a new habit. Thus, I think that we need have regulation to control my behaviour, then we can change my behaviour to be new habit from old habit of behaviour easily. For example, human blood sale is an economic product, due to paying donors for blood would increase supply. Supplies would be provided at a cost advantage in the future, if demand continued to rise. Such as supplies to hospitals for blood will has cost from donors when there are many patients need much blood to use to treat any diseases in any hospitals. Otherwise, if there are not many patients need much blood to use, but there are many donors have effort to provide blood to any hospitals, then it will be economic inefficiency and it is highly wasteful of blood. Thus, the blood donors whose blood supplies of behavior and the cost of blood which will concern to the hospitals patients' numbers of demand, so their behavior and economy has close relationship in the hospital blood demand market.

For shareholder behaviour example, if you hold some shares in a firm that has gone down in value. What do you do? Many people hold on to their shares in this situation, in the hope that they will recoup their losses. Conversely, when shares have gone up in share, people are happy to sell them to realise their gain, A similiar behaviour is also observed for professional traders who tend to hold on to shares with a loss for longer than those with a gain. The traders who exhibit this type of loss to a lesser degree tend to be the more successful ones.

For another example, this is a case where the theory is directly applicable within economic cost-benefit-type analyses that include valuations of no-market products, such as valuations of pollution damage. Policy makers have a choice as to whether-to-accept, and as these may vary by up to a factor, the outcome of such an analysis many well depend on which value is chosen. When a policy maker reasonably has a right to something that might be taken away from them, the willing-to-accept value would be used. On the other hand, when the policy maker only reasonable has a right to the status quo and an improvement is proposed, then the willingness-to-pay is the correct value to use.

What behavioral economic preferences regarding time discounting theory would pay and the conclude that the discounted psychologists have long established utility model, which continues to be that people don't make decisions in widely used by economists, has little the way assumed. In generaly, people are expected to rationally make the best choices given their preferences, independent of how these choices are presented. Therefor more information and choice is always considered good. Using this theory, policy makers should ensure that people always have as much information and as many things to choose between as possible, the process of introducing policy is irrelevant. Ideas from behavioural economic indicate, however that this is not the right approach.

However, we know from experimental economics that more choice and more information can lead to a feeling of helplessness or reduced self-efficiency. Hence, if people hope have better solutions to a probem. Instead, providing people with opportunities for inderstanding, exploration and participation engages powerful motivations for competence, being needed. In summary, people 's self-efficacy increases and they are motivated toward implementing the solutions. i.e. changing their behaviour in a desired way. So, a participatory approach not only improves policy, it also makes to any policy makers more happier. In most cases these principles cannot be used directly as part of any mathematical economics analysis, but highlight situations where this standard analysis will not accurately describe human behaviour and therefore might have unintended consequences when implemented in policy. However, that the policy implications could be quite powerful as the behavioural approach provides quite different lines of analysis to the standard economic model. It is heartening to see policy makers focusing more on the psychology of behaviour when devising policy. So behavioral economics is a relatively new field of economics that attempts to incorporate insights from psychology into economic models and analyses. As above cases seem any policy maker's economic activites which are relative to whose psychology's decision. However, psychologists are often interest in understanding at the level of individual or social group of behaviour, the primary interest in economic is usually in understanding how behaviour and interactions play out in a system to shape economic outcomes. Economists are interested in system-level outcomes, such as the level and path of wages, the effect of taxes on economic output, how rates of savings respond to interest rates etc. However, those economic outcomes depend on complex interactions of individuals. So, behavioural economy concerns to how to judge individual to do the reasonable or right behaviour to hope to get the reasonable economic result as well as it's goal rather to help improve any policy makers to understand their behaviour in ways that allow economists to make better predictions and suggest better economic policies. However, new elements about information processing or individual preferences might impact economic models and analyses.

Is psychology influencing all field of economics? It is possible that behavioral economy needs theoretical contributions and laboratory evidence to support to make any reasonable or right decision to any policy makers. This type of work generally uses existing observational data and estimates relationships between variables of interest by either using naturally occurring variation in the data i.e. natural experiment.

Perhaps more than any other field, behavioral economics has had a large impact on finance to the point that behavior finance is often considered a separate field as opposed to being of behavioral economics. Also, public economic is the study of how government policies in fluence economic markets. A primary emphasis of public economic involves the topic of taxation. Otherwise, the biggest impact that the behavioral approach has had in economic is the analysis of retirement saving to influence any employees' decisions about their retirement savings. However, when employees can do make any active savings choices to prepare their retirement. If employers can assist whose employees to design any methods to allocate fund, then accumuates interest and is tax free until the retirement funds are withdrawn to every retirement employee. The tax advantage make effort to save for retirement.

Behavioral economic is in understanding how individuals do or do not smooth consumption over time. Smoothing consumption is a standard economic models. It suggests that individuals should borrow or save in order to consume a similar amount throughout one's lifetime. For example, a teacher who is paid a salary 12 months a year, who should not spend all whose salary within one year. Rather, the teacher shoud smooth whose consumption over the 12 month period. How to allocate to spend paychecks, food and social security payments which concerns the teacher decide to spend whose salary efficiently. Hence, who needs to plan how he shall spend whose one year salary to be reasonable use in the future. Public economic is to understand how people respond to taxation and social benefit programs. This has been an area that has seen an explosion of behavioral work in recent year. i.e. how taxpayers can experience over-withholding and receive tax refunds from tax department.

Policymakers and insurers are also increasingly turning to psychology for approaches to improve health behavior. Traditionally health-policy focused largely on information provision, assuming that as long as individuals were well informed, their decisions would maximize their health choices. Influential work on the effects of smoking taxes, however, well being of smokers appears to increase with higher taxes to influence health behaviours are not completely rational.

Behavioral economic has also had a small impact on the study of criminal behaviour. For example, individuals are not less likely to commit a crime when who are 18 age and the pubishment of doing so increases dramatically. However, some economists explain the motivations people have for giving to charity and who understand the psychological motivations for charitable giving. So, it seems that charity award giving has probable to reduce 18 age people who choose to do crime behaviour easily because who feel who have effort to assist charity in their life time.

Industrial organization economists study why firms exist and how which function and compete with each other. Insights and psychology and behavioral economics have made a significant contribution to develop that model the interactions of profit maximizing firms with their customers. In fact, firms often need to evaluate whether their products if prices are needed to set what of price of level is the most reasonable and attractive to customers to choose to buy their products. For example, individuals choose cell phone plans with fixed minute allotments and steep charges for going over the minute limits, but frequently exceed their plan limits. This behavior is the best explained by a model in which people overestimate the precision of their demand forecasts. So, cell phone firms need to research how cell phone plans with fixed minute allotments ans steep charges of cell phone call fee charge plan is the most acceptance method to cell phone clients generally. However, cell phone call charge plan and various cell phone product features and the way cell phone clients allocate their limited attention affects cell phone products markets which are external important factors can influence any cell phone clients why who will choose to use the cell phone call plan because any cell phone will be very large durable product to any cell phone consumer after who choose to buy the cell phone product. Hence, who will not often choose to use the old cell phone firm call charge plan if who feel it provides the excellent cell phone call service and reasonable phone call plan to use to compare other cell phone call plans in the cell phone call market. Hence, the cell phone call firm needs to research why consumers need to choose to use which cell phone call plan among of other cell phone call plans in the cell phone call market. Also, researching the cell phone buyers' choice behaviour why who choose to buy the cell phone to use issue, which will have influence to the cell phone buyer why who choose to use the cell phone call charge plan because expensive cell phone is needed to use excellent quality of cell phone call service usually. Otherwise, cheap cell phone is needed to use poor quality of cell phone call service usually. So, cell phone call plan is needed to follow the cell phone quality and price to be used and they ought have direct relationship to influence why the cell phone buyer who chooses to use the cell phone call plan.

Finally, behavioral economic can also apply to be used to labor supply as a motivating in negative or positive labor supply elasticities example. For example, it is possible that taxi drivers work fewer hours when wages are high-consistent with a model of daily income targeting. This finding is that when wages are high (perhaps it is raining and thus it is easy to find people who want a taxi ride), taxi drivers are able to hit their daily target quickly and then go home. However, when wages are low, taxi drivers are not able to hit their target quickly and thus work additional hours in order to hit their target. It means taxi driver's behaviour produce the effect that taxi driver works more when wages are low than when wagers are high. This work has resulted to analyze taxi driver of labor supply decisions with daily reference points in non taxi domains. So, instead of the weather and client numbers and taxi charge factors, the factors of taxi drivers' hours worked and the quality of service is produced is another important factor to influence any taxi drivers' numbers to supply to the taxi market.

Behavioral economic has also influenced the understanding of how staffs can impact worker productivity and job satisfaction. For example, it is possible that poor cooperation can cause worker productivity decreases and it can also cause poor job satisfaction to the worker. So, when working environment can impact productivity, social comparisons can have an impact on job satisfaction as well as the worker's job satisfaction and search intentions are affected by knowing about the salaries of their peers in whose firm. Hence, the worker's positive or negative psychological feeling to whose employers which will have effort to influence whose working performance and productivity to whose firm in possible.

Behavioral economic is increasingly being used in the field of development economics or low income countries. Such as, how Philippines can offer commitment to individuals who wanted to save money in whose country or how Philippines can change to smoking behaviour when commitment devices were offered to Philippine smokers. So, Philippines policy makers need to concern resource scarcity and resource allocation issue to solve how to let its low income level householders can raise to the middle income level to achieve the high income level householders and the low income level householders whose income level is not distant very much.

Analysis whether behavioral economy and psychology which has close relationship.

Finally, I shall analyze whether the relationship between the discipline of behavioral economy and psychology which two branches are totally opposite or if the behavioral theories are only complement that mainstream economics. I think study of economics is the behavior of the complex human beings; this science examines how people choose to act and allocate resources in different market situations. So the economic analysis, is based on the implications that arise from a series of simple assumptions (which are sometimes cited as unrealistic) regarding the human nature. However, in psychological view, the individual is characterized by unlimited rationality and by the ability to follow time consistent, in every situation, his self-interest. In these conditions, behavioral economic attempts to consider a field of analysis in the study of economic phenomena. Because economics deals with the study of human behaviour on the market, it highlights the human character of the science and the fact that, besides of all the patterns and models, the analysis refers to the real individual. It is also behavioural because it attempts to combine approaches from several sciences mainly from economics and psychology, and also from sociology, philosophy, anthropology or biology. This is not an easy mission, in the conditions in which these various disciplines have adopted in time different approaches that became, in many ways, contradictory. So, behavioural economics is that a multidisciplinary appraoch will increase the explanatory power of economics.

On one hand, there are specialists two argue that behavioural economic is a field of economics that continues the hand, there are others who see it as a distinctive school of thought, which proposes a new paradigm. However, behavioural economists propose a multidisciplinary study, criticize certain assumptions on which the traditional model is built (such as rationality and self-interest, in their unlimited form), resource to experiments (the classical method of psychology) to validate some assumptions, propose new theories (such as the prospect theory) and advance different interpretations of the economic behaviour, e.g. how to maximize consumers satisfy their needs. This issue is concerned to concern consumption of pshchology and social economic situation research aspect. Also, I think that behavioural economics can help the economic science by describing more realistically the utility functions of the individuals. This field of study is based rather it is a natural extension of the basic approach. However, it is can be claimed that behavioural economics is also built on the premise that psychology methods and assumptions are equally important. Also, models of behavioural economics, allow the utility to depend on the differences between one's own level and a reference level. People are sensitive to changes and preferences are not stable in time. The vision of behavioural economics concerning the inter-temporal choice (which assumes that individuals prefer immediate gains and delay unpleasant activities) seems to be more appropriate to the human behaviour that the one of the traditional model (which assumes that utility is updated over time).

In conclusion, I shall indicate two theories to explain why economy and psychology has close relationship to influence human do any behavioural economic activities daily. For example, through the prospect theory, behavioural economics adds new parameters to improve the mathematical modelling method, which was advanced by economists for decisions taken under uncertainty.

However, the theory also proposes a slightly different interpretation. The results are interpreted by the individual as positive or negative deviations from a reference point, which has a neutral psychological value. Last but not least, in addressing social preferences, behavioural economics adds parameters that increase the concern of decision-makers to also assess their utility function in relation to others. For another example, the choice theory; secondly there is not a common consensus between the specialists of behavioural economics regarding the variables that should be included; and finally, many variables that affect the behaviour are not quantitative, but qualitative, and cannot be precisely measured. The findings of behavioural economic are relevant and can help the mainstream theory by providing a more realistically base of study. However, this argument has contributed to the development of behavioural economics, because there are a large number of phenomena that cannot be entirely emplained by the mainstream economics. So, why in the beginning, I indicated why behavioural economics does not imply the totally exclusion of the neoclassical approach and the most studies in this area try to provide a more realistic base of the standard theory. In the concluding, I believe that in time, behavioural economic models will replace the simplified ones, based on unlimited rationality. Also, economists have provided a great importance to the quantitative structures, departing from the human nature. However, behavioural economics can become truly revolutionary only it it will always be receptive and will provide a critical insight to their own theories and perspectives, and especially the ones regarding the aspects that they reproach to the traditional economic theory. However, I also feel that the individual's behaviour on the market is determined only be economic factors. In brief, individual choices and, by this, the demand variation are explained only and the variations in the prices of products/ services and the available personal income. Am inportant discussion in the field of determine directly the economic behaviour of an individual (like the sociological and psychological of factors) are actually active elements in the process the reshaping of the utility functions. Finally, in my view, I believe that the conduct of the market phenomena, as it occurs in reality. In this sense, the research of behavioural economics aims to see how the neoclassical model could be improved, using mainly psychology concepts. Although, there are some specialists who argue that behavioural economics can be an alternative to the neoclassical theory.

Most findings, of my study conducted in this book, modify some of standard economical assumptions, in order to provide a greater psychological realism. However, the additions proposed by behavioural economists simply recognize the human limitations on (mentally) calculations, will and self-interest. So, I think psychology and economy has close relationship to influence any policy makers or decision makers to do any economic psychology daily. Because the purpose of economics is to better understand and explain the conduct of the economic activities as which occur in reality. Otherwise, human being is complex and its behaviour and constitution is studied by all the social sciences. Consequently, multi and interdisciplinary approaches can bring real benefits to the economic science, by providing a more realist foundation to cause any policy makers or decision makers how to decide to make any behaviours or economic activities by behavioural economic activities support daily.

THREE

THE DIFFERENT ASPECTS OF POLICY PREVENT THE ECONOMIC RECESSION CRISIS OCCURRENCE

What is Human development policy.

The current economic crisis has affected all aspects of life resulting in political instability, personal financial troubles and a growing number of business bankruptcies. How to use effective policy to prevent the economic crisis threats. I shall indicate that governments ought to consider these different aspects to prevent the economic recession crisis occurrence to threaten to influence whose social economic growth.

On the human development hand, examples of which include high quality education and health systems aspects. Different country's government ought to concern, due to it can support the productivity of an economy by providing healthy and highly trained individuals. Because of the country has good human development strategy, then it can use talent labors to assist its economic growth and good governance practices by governments easily. It seems that human development, good governance and economic growth has close relationship, so it can reduce the economic recession during times of crisis occurrence. It means that human development can influence economic growth. Economic development implies both the improvement of people's health education and general well being and the presence of positive economic indicaties, such as economic growth and low unemployment with economic development, people will have better education and healthcare and be more productive. Better human development nations tend to have lower crime rates and greater political strategy than less human development nations.

Whether is it a consequence of human development to prevent economic recession? It will be an important resource to influence economic growth. How does this human development public policy solve economic crisis? Whether can government use of fiscal policy, such as human development to assist economic stabilization to promote growth and the increase of the capital income efficiency? A key issue relates to the effect of how to use public expenditure and its financing to spend human development on effects of fiscal policy by using a time series approach. A general model that includes expenditure on education and health, which influences human capital, expenditure and health administration, public investment and transfers and consumption of public products four kinds of expenditure. The model can be used to explore and impact of human development expenditure used on long run per capita income. Debt and external and financing are also possible to be spent to human development expenditure in the general model. So, the public expenditure on the long run per capita income can be explored for low, lower, middle and upper-middle income countries policy that is needed to be esimated how to spend for each aspect of human development expenditure to assist to every country's economy development.

What is time series perspective on business cycle stages to pursue for growth and human development strategies.

A time series perspective on economic growth may be more useful to pursue for growth and human development strategies. A time series can allow to pursue time series studies for particular countries or country groups at particular stages of economic growth. It can allow for a more specific micro behavior of economic agents. In general, any country has three income groups, such as low income, lower-middle income and upper middle income groups. Also, any country may have these four types of public expenditure for human development which including: enhancing education and building up of human capital, public investment to finance general market and subsistence production, e.g. transportation system, such as roads, bridges, harbors, water supply, sanitation, health and care and education.

A 2005 year study had been carried by Dimonson, Marsh & Staunton, which performed an analysis is stock returns in 53 countries, going back to 1900 year for 17 countries, did not find evidence of a significant long term positive relationship between GDP growth rates and equity returns. Also the analysis from Schroders Economics team found that over the past sixty years, there has tended to be a positive relationship between GDP growth and equity market returns during the recovery, expansion and slowdown phases of the traditional business cycle. This relationship has traditionally broken down during the recession phase. The Schroders economics team also indicated a traditional business cycle model, which has four stages. In the beginning, it is slowdown stage. It means output above trend, growth decelerating and inflation rising. Next is recession stage. It means output below trend, growth developing, inflation falling. Then, it is recovery stage. It means output below trend, growth decelerating, inflation falling. Finally, it is expansion stage, it means output above trend growth accelerating, inflation is rising. The economic team also suggested the traditional business cycle model: In the slowdown stage, GDP growth is positive, but falling, inflation is high and rising, so policy strategy is tight recommended in the recession stage, GDP growth is negative and falling, inflation is falling. So, policy strategy is loosening recommended. In the recovery stage, GDP growth is negative and rising, inflation is low and falling, so policy strategy is loose recommended. Finally, the expansion stage, GDP growth is positive and rising, inflation is rising, so policy strategy is tightening recommended. It seems that governments ought concern the business cycle period to evaluate themselves country GDP growth to achieve the most effective policy to adopt to achieve different human development policies to invest to present economic recession crisis occurrence. Usually, in the recovery and expansion phases of the business cycle, the stock market tends to perform well as rising GDP and earnings growth drives positive excess returns on equity. In the slowdown phase, inflation is still high and monetary policy remains tight, resulting in s difficult environment for corporations. reducing earnings and stock valuations tends to result in negative excess returns for equities: declining GDP growth is therefore usually matched with poor equity performance. It also explained that during the recession phase, there is often GDP growth is falling, but the excess return on equity tends to be positive. Historically, falling inflation and an accompanying loosening of monetary policy is needed to rise re-rating.

Thus, it seems the business cycle and human development policy has close relationship. During in the slowdown stage, GDP growth is positive, but falling, inflation is high and rising, then the country's government ought spend less expenditures to human development because GDP growth is stable growth. Otherwise, during it is recession stage or recovery stage, it means output below trend, growth developing, inflation falling. Then the country's government ought spend more to invest to any human development needs to prepare to raise whose labor productivity and GDP growth. Finally, during the expansion stage, GDP growth is positive and rising, inflation is rising. Then the country's government can spend less expenditures to invest human development. Thus, any country's government ought concern what is whose country's business cycle stage to arrange to spend more or less expenditures to achieve its human development policy in different business cycle stages.

What is quantitative evidence to review policy to reduce the threats from economic recession risk occurrence.

- Regulatory management method

Nowadays, political scientists began to apply quantitative methods to classify and measure political interactions. In general, any countries‘ policies that maximize growth are optimal that cares solely about pure " capitalists". The greater, the inequality of wealth and income, the higher rate of taxation and the lower growth. It shows that inequality in land and income ownership is negatively with subsequent economic growth. Many economists have tried to explain lower growth rates and unemployment with a growing tax burden in many developed countries. Although, the impact of taxes on growth can be observed both from the aspect of efficiency and aspect of changes in equity that taxes introduce to economy.
I shall indicate how to apply quantitative evidence to review policy to reduce the threats from economic recession risk occurrence. In fact, economic or welfare outcomes to changes in regulatory policy has close relationship to be suggested outcome indicate to reduce risk face economic recession occurrence to any countries. Every country government ought design to gather quantitative data to prepare any policy implementation to support mutual learning and best practice in different societal and market conditions. The goal is to help countries to build better government systems and implement policies at both national and regional level that lead to sustainable economic and social development.

The critical public policy challenge is to ensure that the expected economic benefits from regulatory changes are both achieved and outweigh any economic cost imposed. I shall indicate evidence on the outcomes of regulatory policies to help policymakers how design regulatory measures that work better. This method is called "regulatory management". This regulatory management study suggests some conclusions to any policymakers. Firstly, poorly designed policy regulation can not raise economic activities and ultimately reduce economic growth. Secondly, it is impossible between a regulatory policy change and the impact on economic outcomes, such as economic growth is from statistic method easily. Third, the reliance on economic recession analysis to investigate the relationship across countries between regulatory variables and economic outcomes may not be readily applicable to any countries and may not always be expressed in economic values. It is particularly useful in developing countries regulatory policy measures for recommendation to policymakers only. Fourth, most quantitative studies deal with the costs of regulation and give little or no attention to quantifying the benefits of regulation. For the policymaker, it is important to compare the estimated costs of regulation. Any policy regulation is intended to correct market failures and assist to economic efficiency and growth. The public policy aims to reduce socially unacceptable income and wealth distributions or it can satisfy expectation that the public should have access to certain products and services, e.g. health care and education irrespective of ability to pay, such as merit products. Some of regulation, that governments need to concern, e.g. of property rights, company law, law of contract etc. and regulation can provide important economic and social, including environmental benefits. Of course, those benefits need to be set against the costs.

Because regulations are the operations of effective economies and societies to market rules, e.g. law of contract and protecting property rights and the rights of citizens. It seems regulatory management is important to influence any policies can be achieved effectively, due to one good regulation can supervise the leader's behavior and otherwise one bad regulation can not supervise the leader's behavior, even it can not assist the country economic growth for long term. So, any leader needs to concern how to use quantitative evidence to review policy if who hopes whose policy's regulations are achieved effectively.

At the same time, economic, environmental and welfare pressures raise the demand for regulation above minimum needed for operating a market economy to prepare to face the economic recession occurrence. So, evidence on the outcomes of regulatory policies should help policymakers design regulatory measures that work better. Similarly, evidence on the success or failure of regulation can be used for public accountability purposes. Regulatory policy defines as the process by which government, when identifying a policy objectives, decides whether to use regulation as a policy instrument and proceeds to draft and adopt a regulation through evidence based decision making. The strategy shall commit governments to remain a regulatory management system, articulating regulatory policy goals, and the impacts of regulation on competitiveness and economic growth. For example, regulation, such as employment law or competition law, the regulation of employment law is applied to control any employers' behaviors to give the fair treatment to whose employees and to protect employees' benefits. Besides the regulation of competition law is applied to control the fair competition in market. Why this regulations has direct relationship to economy growth. An identifiable economy theory of specific regulatory policies, e.g. administrative simplification and specific economic and welfare outcomes, e.g. high economic growth. The result is a series about the impact of regulatory management on economic indicators. There can be set out as a causal. Thus regulation can be supportive of market transactions and may result in significant economic, social and environmental benefits. At the same time, ill-designed regulation can have appreciable economic costs, leading to the concept of regulatory burden. In particular, good regulation can reduce the chance of lower economic growth or GDP occurrence, damage investment and competitiveness. But, it has also weakness, such as regulatory costs may act as a barrier to entry into industry in the form of set up cost, e.g. installing equipment to meet health and safety laws and on going annual cost, e.g. preparing returns and facilities inspections.

However, regulatory can be unduly costly to comply with administrator and enforce, but it simplification can reduce the regulatory burden. For example, regulation may not only affect the behavior of those targeted by a rule (direct effects), but invoke behavioral change in the economy (indirect effects). Whether regulation can support governments to avoid or reduce the threats of economic recession occurrence, it depends on the leader's concern how to use quantitative evidence to review policy before who decides to implement which kinds of regulatory management methods.

In recent year, some countries had considered how to achieve policy field with a view to introducing better regulation. The aim is to ensure that regulation occurs only when it does improve social welfare and that regulatory changes do, so with the minimum net cost or maximum net benefit to society. For a policy making perspective, it is important to appreciate how and why a regulatory achievement can be expected to result in a particular impact. Causal chain analysis is a technique for explaining the way in which a caused regulatory results in an economic impact. By helping to understand the how and why questions, regulatory impact, so causal chain analysis can provide policymakers, with relevant information on the consequences of their policy decisions. It seems that regulation can lead economic improvements, such as higher GDP growth, higher productivity, move business start ups. etc. Due to the causal chain analysis relates to each component separately. So, any decision maker hopes to achieve better regulation, who needs time to attempt to different regulations to achieve whose policies every year. Then, who can review why whose policy can not improve whose country's economic growth as well as to attempt to find reasons how to apply better regulatory to achieve better policy to improve its country's economic growth. It seems review regulatory policy which ought to concern to any decision maker, if who wanted to achieve better regulatory policy to raise economic and welfare gains every year.

Whether it has relationship between political instability and national economic performance.

Tax policy influences, during polictical instability environment.

Whether it has relationship between political instability and national economic performance. By past history indicated that the depletion of resource during wars may be one reason why some countries fail to sustain adequate economic growth. However, because economic growth affects a population's well being, this question concerning how was related to growth is important from a policy perspective. So, civil wars can influence any country's economic growth because war can cause the falling changes in a country's physical and human capital as well as lacking technology supporting can reduce GDP per capita to be country during war occurs. For example, during war does noe occur, then trade liberalization, democracy, government stability and a legal system that strongly protects private property rights enhance growth.

During the political instability is occurring, whether tax policy can assist economic growth and social welfare growth. On of central questions in macroeconomics and public policy is how changes in tax policy affect economic activity and social welfare. Consequently, it is possible that sometimes, taxing leads to inefficiency in economy. Whether can taxes stimulate people to change their behavior. For example, the person could either work so hard as before introduction of taxes and reduce whose spending, or work more and spend less time at leisure, thus not needing to reduce spending substantially. However, the inefficiency is caused by taxes, will be presented with a simple supply and demand diagram. In other words, taxes have impact on the amount of supply and demand for products and services. The purpose of understanding of the impact of taxes on welfare, the decrease in welfare of consumers and producers should be compared with the tax revenue by the country. Such an analysis will show that the decrease in consumers' and producers' welfare exceeds the tax revenue collected by the country. The loss of welfare that takes place after introduction of taxes (a part of which belongs to no one either to a consumer or producer, nor to the country) represents a weight loss or excess tax burden as a degree of inefficiency that taxes introduce to economy. However, full understanding of weight loss requires a detailed tax burden of analysis is needed to governments. What determines the size of the heavy weight loss to tax? A higher price elasticity of demand curve, or a higher price elasticity of supply curve can lead to a higher weight loss to tax. The more elastic the curves are, the higher is the inefficiency that taxes introduce to the market. The fact is taxes introduce heavy weight loss to the economy because which stimulate people to change their behavior. Since elasticity of supply and demand is a measure of change in the behavior of consumers and producers in relation to change of prices , it also determines the rate of market distortion. The more elastic supply and demand curves, the higher is the heavy weight loss. Another important determinant of the size of heavy weight loss is the tax rate. When price elasticity of supply and demand is the same, heavy weight loss is low when taxes are low and it grows when which both grow. Indeed, heavy weight loss grows faster than most taxes: we can sat that the size of heavy weight loss provided that production costs are constant is equal to 1/2 (elasticity / product quantity), where it is tax rate. Elasticity is price elasticity of demands, product is price of Q is quantity of products.

What is tax saving and investment relationship

What is taxation of savings and investment relationship? Taxes can reduce economic growth by affecting savings and investment. The higher the proportion of income that is being saved and invested, the higher will be the future income level, In other words, through its impact on the amount of the income being saved or invested, taxation policy has a crucial effect on the future level of income per capita. The impact of taxes on saving of individuals and companies, investment in fixed capital and investment risk is briefed represented below: How impact of taxes on savings of individual? The gross savings in private sector and accumulated in households and companies. However, a large past of the gross savings is used for covering depreciation and is needed for the existing capital. The net savings, consisting of savings to householders and earnings of companies, represent the real potential, available for new investments. If all householders would save the same proportion of income, then the impact of income tax on the total savings would be the same, regardless of the pattern of the distribution of tax burden to individuals. But, wealthy individuals shall save more than poor citizens. So, it is expected that the tax collected from higher tax brackets create more burden on savings than the ones collected from lower tax brackets. Consequently, on individual tax behavior view, a more progressive income tax seems to be creating a heavier burden on savings than a less progressive tax system. So I suggest a less progressive income tax policy will encourage more savings of individuals. However, it is a only assumption, it has another factors to influence citizen's tax behavior: such as, a varies during a life cycle in youth and in old age, it is much lower saving than in middle are when income in highest and when people save for education of their children for a house or flat and for the old age to prepare retirement. So, tax policy is not considered by firms or policymakers in isolation from other aspects of site selection including benefits from public products which are needed to use by citizens, e.g. gardens, swimming pools, entertainment facilities etc. different public facilities.

What is educational development policy

On education aspect, many of the assumptions which are attempted to rationalize the process of educational development have been criticized or abandon. However, the education quality role of different educational regulation, the choice of financing methods, the examination and certification procedures or various other regulation and incentive structures will influence educational effect to satisfy public needs. Thus, educational policy makers need to satisfy public needs. Moreover, educational policymakers also need to concern any new policy making environment which will seriously constrain their attempts to ensure the early discussion of planning considerations as part of the education policy making process. So, every country's environment factor will influence every educational policymaker's individual decision.

As defined, policy represents decisions that are designed to guide (including to constrain future decisions or to initiate and guide the implementation of previous decisions). It is this time bound nature of policy and of policy making that makes it is such a critical concern for the educational planner. However, the failure of the traditional planning models and the recognition of the lack of nationality that can occur in policy making there combined to create an atmosphere of pessimism among some educationalists.

To capture the details of the decision making process of any educational planning itself, an analytical framework is presented that goes beyond the initial decision point to examine both the preceding actions (contextual assessment, technical analysis and the generation, valuation and selection of policy options) and the subsequent activities (planning and conducting implementation, impact assessment and where appropriate, design). Thus, the framework covers the full policy planning process, but with a focus on the facilitating and constraining effects that policy decisions and how they were derived and have no the choices available to educational planners.

There are two ways of value to educational planners. First, the methodology of the framework and conclusions of the any one of educational case studies should help in the analysis of current educational policies and decision making procedures (an analysis of policy). So, it is a present method to gather current data from current case studies to make the update conclusions to achieve any any of eductional policies. Otherwise, Second, the another framework can be applied to have evaluation of proposed policies and used to forecast policy outcomes and the probability of successful implementation, given the country of fiscal and management capacity, political commitment etc. So, this framwork is a futuer predict educational method to gather data how to get the recommedation to achieve the effiective quality of educational policy in the future.

Educational policies can be lower differ in terms of scope, complexity, decision environment, range of choices and decision criteria. Any educational policy decision deals with large scale policies and broad resource allocation will have these questions to need to answer. For example, on strategic view, how can we provide basic education at a reasonable cost to meet equity and efficiency objectives? On multi program view, should resources be allocated to university level education? On program view, how would occupational training centre be designed and provided across the country? On issue specific view, should graduated of rural universities be allowed to transfer to any one of city area universities to study easily? On the psychological view, some researches indicated behavioral economics with emotions has close relationship to any policy making, such as educational policy. More recently, economists as well as psychologists who are specifically interested in decision making have begun to take greater concerning emotional influence. So, it seems any policy decision making whose any one of final policy decisions which is influenced to achieve or not achieve from their emotion indirectly. Usually, then an economy is doing well, there is less incentive to encourage new entrepreneurial firms if the country's citizens and firms have enough jobs supply and have enough labor supply in the job market. It seems that good economic growth country will have this question why it needs to take a risk on something new. So, emotions have close link to our societies to influence any country's citizens real needs and entrepreneurs' business aim to develop any societies' economy to be grown. So, any countries' policies decision makers ought concern whose enterprises and citizens whose real needs, then who can attempt to choose what methods of policies to assist whose countries' economy development more effective.

What is national environment policy

National environment concept influences economic growth

On natural environment view, whether every country's natural environment has close relationship to assist its economic growth. The natural environment is central to economic activity and growth, providing the resources, we need to produce products and services and absorbing and processing unwanted by-product in the form of pollution add waste. So, environment assets contribute to managing risks to economic and social activity helps to regulate flood risks, regulating the local climate both air quality and temperature and maintaining the supply of clean water and resources both.

Government's role is to send clear signals and set a long term policy framework in order to provide businesses with the certainty who need to make investments in low carbon and resource efficient technologies. It is also essential that government listens to and works with business, so that policies are designed in a way that avoids unnecessary burdens and removes potential barriers to success. So, the natural environment plays an important role in supporting economic activity. It contributes: directly, by providing resources and raw materials, such as water, timber and minerals that are required as inputs for the production of products and services and indirectly, through services provided by ecosystems including carbon water purification, managing flood risks and nutrient cycling.

The relationship between economic growth and the environment is complex. Several different drivers come into play, including the scale and composition of the economy, particularly the share of services in GDP as opposed to primary industries and manufacturing and changes in technology that have the potential to reduce the environmental impacts of production and consumption decisions when also driving economic growth. In fact, economic growth involves the combinations of different types of capital to produce products and services these include; produced capital, such as machinery, buildings and roads; human capital, such as skills and knowledge, natural capital, e.g. raw materials are extract from the earth, carbon and services is provided by forests and social capital, such as institutions and ties within communities. So, government needs to concern that national resources can not be extracted too much to lead our natural capital is lacked to produce any products or to provide services in the future.

In particular, market failure in the provision and use of environmental resources mean that natural assets would be over-used in the absence of government intervention. These market failures arise from the public product characteristics of the natural environment, external costs and benefits, where the use of a resource by one party has impacts on others, difficulties in capturing the full benefits of business investment in environmental research and development, and information failure. Market failures may include water quality and to vehicle emissions to influence human's body health. So, any countries' government needs to achieve these policies which concerns on environmental protection aspect to achieve its public spending and technology policy, such as on developing flood infrastructure, supporting low carbon technologies electric vehicles. Also on the information provision and other policies to address barriers to influence consumer's behavior change, such as product labelling policies and policies to increase take up of resource efficiency measures to provide environment protection. So, effective environmental policy is likely to require and the use of multiple instruments, each tackling to require part of the problem when avoiding duplication and unnecessary regulatory burdens. Also, pricing environmental inputs can correctly help any businessmen to manage how to use natural resources effectively.

Environmental policy aims to reduce how the economy and the businesses are to adverse environmental events, by reducing environmental risk both. For example, not just investments that facilities emissions reductions to avoid dangerous climate change, but also those investments that help to economy adapt to climate impacts already locked in by past and current emissions. The natural environment plays a key role in our economy, as a direct input into production and through the many services it provides. Environmental resources, such as minerals and fossil fuels directly facilities the production of products and services. The environment provides other services that enable economic activity, such as carbon, filtering air and soil formation. It is also vital for against flood risk, and soil formation. It is also vital for our wellbeing, providing us with recreational opportunities, improving our health and much more. Human wellbeing in a complex and diverse concept, determined by a wide-range of factors including levels of income absolute and relative, health status, educational attainment, housing conditions and environmental quality.

National capital contributes to economic output through two main channels: directly as an input to the process of economic activity, indirectly through its effect on the productivity of the other factors of production. However, natural capital is as a direct input to wealth creation, which can provide the raw materials for economic production of products the raw materials for economic production of products and services, it includes non renewable resources like, fossil fuels, minerals metal extracted from the natural environment to produce energy, machinery, consumer products, renewable resources, natural processes or own reproduction. Why do our governments need to concern environmental policy? The reasons include natural areas provide global life support functions, including climate regulation and regulation of the chemical composition of the atmosphere and oceans. When natural areas play a role in the maintenance of life essential services, it is difficult to evaluate and demonstrate the contribution that particular habitat types or areas make. Water regulation can reduce flood and storm protection and prevent damage. Natural processes can also provide water quality benefits, pollution includes the removal of nutrients and pollutants from water, filtering of dust from the air, and providing noise. Waste sink includes all non recycled waste is produced by economic activity. In the absorptive capacity of the atmosphere, the oceans and the soil protection, such as many wetland habitats, provides benefits by preventing soil loss. Nutrient cycling includes storage, processing and acquisition of nutrients essential for plant growth in ecological process and waste decomposition, naturally occurring micro-organisms provide benefits through their ability to break down organization matter and speed up the process of waste decomposition.

How government policy can influence on capturing private investment.

How government policy can influence on capturing private investment. Whether government policy can attract foreign direct investment or different countries. Increased levels of trade and foreign direct investment worldwide, a cause or effect of the closer interdependence of world economies are a reality. What is the relationship among these private, public and civil society sectors? Every country contribution is to add to the public policy stream to understand how the main forces in society operate and cooperate in promoting foreign direct investment. Governments have always been concerned about how to position themselves in an increasingly competitive market for a limited supply of investment resources. Why should a multi-national firm choose one country attraction ? e.g. tax breaks, profit repatriation, low domestic content requirement etc. How can one country strategically position itself against others? Is there an association between pro-social public policy and levels of global private investment? We are particularly interested in those economies in earlier stages of development, where pro-social policies are a rarer phenomenon, as they provide a testing for our hypotheses. What is the relationship between the ability of an host country to attract private investment and the quality of pubic policies affecting the life of its citizens? Are pro-social host government policies in host countries linked to higher inward flows of foreign direct investment to that country?

There has three country level macroeconomic indicators to represent different facets of size: Host country economy growth rate, host country population and host country's rate of inflation. GDP growth, the annual percent change of output in real terms percent, reflects the strength of local economy and the increase in the size of domestic market, opening the door to large sales and high profits. Thus, higher GDP growth should generally be attracted to larger foreign investment. Population is another indicator of market size. It attracted to foreign investment with both large populations and high GDP per capita. So, encouraging immigration and birth rate can attract more foreign investment. Inflation enters the regression as a proxy for macroeconomic stability and as a reflection of the internal or external shocks suffered by the economy during the period under study, which may attract potential inflation sign of internal economic instability and of the host government's inability to maintain consistent monetary policy. It will influence foreign investment confidence. So stable inflation of the host country can increase confidence to let more foreign investment.

How fiscal policy can affect medium to long term economic growth. It is difficult to measure the factors and to determine causality with certainty, between fiscal policy and economic growth relationship. Fiscal reforms are needed to concern structural reforms, e.g. labor or trade and supportive macroeconomic policies. At the macro level, fiscal policy can help to ensure macroeconomic stability, an essential prerequisite for growth at the micro level, tax and expenditure policies can boost growth by altering work and investment incentives, promoting human capital accumulation and enhancing total factor productivity. For example, combining fiscal reforms, e.g. sealing up infrastructure investment when improving the public investment process can increase their effectiveness. Complementary reforms, such as liberalizing trade of fiscal reforms by promoting savings, stimulating investment and not lacking productivity gains, policy uncertainty and high levels of public debt large fiscal deficits reduce aggregate savings in the economy and may lead to inflation, high interest rates and balance of payments pressures, with negative growth consequences. Policymakers need to concern the durability and equity. For example, Netherland, an expenditure cut of 15% of GDP between 1982 year and 2000 year created room sector job-creation. At the same time, both countries managed to avert adverse consequence on income inequality. In advanced and emerging market economies, age related spending on public persons and health care accounts for a large share of government spending (40% and 30%, respectively, IMF, 2014 f). Otherwise, Poland shifted from a financially defined benefit system to an actuarially solvent defined contribution system, and Germany put its pension system on a more sound financial by linking pension benefits to the old age dependency ratio, tightening access to early retirement and rising the statutory retirement age. In health care, Germany and the Netherlands introduced a combination of macro and micro level reforms to contain cost and enhance efficiency, including price controls on pharmaceuticals, higher co-payment and contributions and budget.

Whether national leadership and economic growth has close relationship.

Whether national leadership and economic growth has close relationship. Leaders have strongest effects in autocracies, where who appear to substantially influence both economic growth and the evolution of political institutions. I shall indicate to explain why substantial roles for individual leaders and national institutional change, which can further influence the growth environment. In the past, examinations of the fundamental causes of growth debate between institutions, culture and geography, which typically operate without reference to the actions of particular personalities. However, economists may imagine leaders indirectly as policymakers, leaders, themselves are rarely the subject of focus.

The constraints imposed on leaders from electoral pressures, opposition parties, independent legislatures and judiciaries all vary across countries. To the extent that the authority embedded in formal institutional rules and the authority embedded in individuals act as substitutes, the increasing visibility of institutional variation in explaining paths may indirectly motivate leaders' behaviors. Theories of economic growth that emphasize public products, e.g. education, health, public entertainment facilities, such as parks, swimming pools etc. Also, national policies include international trade, monetary policy and fiscal policy etc. or all suggest possibly important roles for a national leader. However, identifying a causative effect of leaders on economic growth is challenging. Even, if it has relationship between particular leaders and particular economic growth in particular economic environment. However, it may be that growth changes drive leadership changes, without a causative effect of leaders. Assumption that a leader quality is independently, it seems the leader has no influence on economic growth. An important additional assumption is that the leader effects are strongest in autocratic settings, especially in the absence of political parties or legislatures to support the leader's any personal view points to achieve any regulations to influence economic growth effectively. These results point to an important effect between institutions and leader individuals in understanding economic growth paths. However, it seems institutions can influence the impact of national leaders behaviors and that national leaders can also influence the path of institutions. If leaders can influence economic growth, then may further these questions are raised: Do leaders act to obstruct economic growth or do they actively promote it? In this view, leaders can be actively good for economic growth, e.g. by investing in public products, choosing pro-growth trade policies, or overcoming national scale coordination problems. However, related questions of how leaders influence growth are related to the role of national policies in explaining growth. If policies might be well matter, even if leaders do not, if national policies care the expression of broader social forces. So, it seems national policies can also influence economic growth, instead of the leader's personal quality. So, it can get this question and conclusion. When asking how do we make poor countries rich? The unexplained, non-deterministic past of economic growth variation becomes especially relevant and given the results about leadership, more within reach.

Whether behavioral economy and psychology knowledge can be applied to assist economic development.

Whether behavioral economy can be applied to inform and develop policy effectively. Such policies stress that changing the way choices are presented or changing the environment in which decisions are made, can substantially alter behavior. Ideas from behavioral economics have helped to develop the traditional economic choice framework, in which people are assumed to make choices that are rational, self interested and consistent. Some of the most important behavioral insights for tax and benefit policy include: Faced with complicated decisions, people may make choices, which are often approximately optimal, in that who maximize welfare, but might in some cases lead to poor choices. There is evidence that how choices are presented affects outcomes. The environment in which decisions are made would provide cues to make particular choices or made could provide cues to make particular choices, or some aspects of the choice problem may be more or less influence to consumers. When any policy relates to income and spending, or it is label money for another can affect what people choose to do with it. Individuals appear to care not just about their own outcomes, but also about those of others. This might be because people derive value from fairness and cooperation. These motivations could give intrinsic incentive to make particular choices. It is possible that providing extrinsic incentives, such as taxes, fines or rewards could be crowded our desirable behavior.

Consumers may have to exercise costly self control to make certain choices, such as eating health foods or giving up smoking. Commitment devices to help overcome self control problems are therefore values, for example, raising the cost of tempting choices, increasing cigarette taxes, say: when making choices with uncertain outcomes, people will do a number of behavioral features. Such as, attaching subjective decision weights to each outcome and these may differ from objective measures of probability. Usually, outcomes are measured against a reference point, relative to the reference point are felt more strongly than equivalent gains. When welfare increases and ever bigger gains falls, as the welfare cost is from ever bigger losses, then people will appear to be risk seekers when welfare cost comes to cause social loss. How people value the future changes with the passage of time. Usually people hope to earn immediate rewards in present than distant rewards in the future. This means that people make plans who find it hard to achieve. People may also make choices under the assumption that their preferences won't change in the future. So, for policymakers those biases have important implications for why behavior change interventions may be necessary.

Behavioral insights provide new reasons to intervene, issues of self control, for example, making failure, where outcomes are come from the perspective of either individuals or society or both usually. As a common failure is the case of externalities, when individual choices generate costs or benefits for others. Since, these are not taken into account in private decision making, which are come from a social perspective, there is too much or too little of the activity. In this case, taxes or subsidies can help private and social incentives. So, behavioral economical concept can be suggested these important insights for externalities, such as private decisions are closer to the social optimum, reducing the need for correcting taxes or subsidies. It seems that taxes or subsidies will affect to change people's behaviors if social preferences are important. Externalities can arise not just because of how someone affects the well being of others, but also through how decisions made today affect the individual in the future. This is known as an internality. Taxes or subsidies policies both can influence people's present behaviors to be changed and future behaviors will be influenced to be changed from whose present behaviors in societies. Thus, policymakers can not neglect this policy of method to attempt to solve any social challenge nowadays.

Finally, why behavioral economy can assist policy development. Behavioral economy is a science, includes psychology, economics, finance and sociology to understand human behavior and decision making. Behavioral economics recognizes that constraints in time and mental resources prevent us from optimally evaluating every decision. To deal with our limitations, so we rely on mental decision to judge our face of uncertainty, but we can be leaded to predictably irrational behaviors from behavioral economical concept. As government agencies enact laws and regulations that are focused in the society. They often rely on restrictions, incentives or public information campaigns in order to change citizen behavior. When well intentioned, those traditional approaches can be accepted. For example, regulations that can be supported to financial advisers disclose conflicts of interest have led to achieve any final results. Disclosures can increase pressures on advisees to comply with the advice provided and in some cases increase greater perceptions of trust rather than the evaluation of biased advice. Similarly, tax incentives can increase retirement savings rates which have had limited impact. Researchers studying the impact of concluded that such policies are an expensive way of encouraging new savings.

On the one hand, governments ought engage their citizens to do any action, whose action is influenced by behavioral economics to discover how behavioral economics can be provided powerful insights into human motivation and behavior. As different countries‘ government experiments are more from academic laboratories to the real world. So, it is a kind of method to be applied to assist any countries' governments how to use effective policy to improve people's lives. For example, designing what is the best reasonable taxes, subsidies, incentives or educational campaigns level at the rate, donations and retirement savings rates as well as healthy food product label consumption of selection etc. strategic policies which are related how to apply behavioral economy to analyze or experiment to gain the better choice among of them. On the another hand, Economic agents ought attempt to spend time to gather data to choose to do the best decision, but not perfectly national ones. Also economic research should be used reasonable assumptions about agents' cognitive actives. So, economic models should take predictions that are consistent with micro-level data on decisions, including experimental evidence. Moreover, economists ought spend much time to learn from psychologists. Behavioral economists now routinely combine experimental data, field data and theory to construct their arguments. As behavioral economic continues to gain acceptance, behavioral economists will increasingly find themselves participating in policy discussions. As policy has the ability to do good or to create great mislead, depending on who, leader is in charge of making the rules. Indeed in some cases the findings of behavioral economists suggest that active policies may be quite harmful. Successful policy analysis should be concerned the motives of private actors, e.g. consumers and firms and the public or governmental actors need to design formulate and enforce policy with cooperation to regulators, bureaucrats, politicians. So, policy analysis must also be carefully concerned the institutional environment in which these private and public actors interact, e.g. , market, elections and bureaucracies. However, any bad decision making is caused from bounded rationality, slow learning, framing and lack of self control with those effects in mind, one might conclude that government can easily improve consumers' welfare by paternalistically helping consumers make better decisions. Such paternalistic policies can improve consumer welfare by enhancing an individual's maximizing whose own welfare. So, this stands in contrast to most public policies, which address externalities or public products problems that arise because of interactions among economic agents. To conclude, psychology and behavioral economy and public policy which have close relationship, As if the national leader had health psychology, then who will have more possible to achieve good behavior to perform to decide how to achieve any the best public policies to raise growth to make welfare to whose citizens. So any policymakers ought need to concern how to listen to behavioral scientists to let them to give any recommendation how to improve or review or revise whose psychological challenges to let them have more effort to decide how to choose to do the right decision effectively. Because the relationship between psychology and behavioral science has more generally to influence public policy which is particularly painful and frustrating of the success for any similar policy recommendations. Hence, economics and psychology indeed can provide policymakers with vital tools to develop the best policy to solve any social challenges. Consequently, it seems the leader's psychology will influence whose behavioral performance to be decided to choose to do the more correct policy to influence economic development more easily. It also means that one leader's psychology is an important factor to influence any social economic development directly for long term. So who can not neglect to concern whether whose psychological mind is right or wrong to already to make any decisions to plan any policies before whose any polices are implemented. Because the leader's psychology will influence whose behavior is more correct to decide to decide how to do any policies effectively.

Reference

Dimson, Marsh & Staunton, London Business School (2005) In The Global Investment Returns Year Book, ABN Amro.

Fiscal Policy And Long Term Growth, International Monetary Fund, IMF policy papers, Washington, D.C. Available from April, 2015, http://www.imf.org/external/pp/ppindex.aspx.

Printed by Libri Plureos GmbH in Hamburg,
Germany